Your Deaf Child

A GUIDE FOR PARENTS

Sixth Printing

HELMER R. MYKLEBUST, ED.D.

Professor of Audiology
Northwestern University

With a Foreword by
HALLOWELL DAVIS, M. D.

This book is written for *parents of deaf children.* Not many books of this sort have been written. It will open the eyes of many to the *happy possibilities that lie ahead* for deaf children, if parents really understand their child's problems and if they deal with them according to Dr. Myklebust's sound advice.

WHAT DEAFNESS MEANS • PARENTS' GROUPS
CAUSES AND TYPES OF DEAFNESS • SPEECH
YOUR ATTITUDES AND WHAT THEY MEAN
HEARING AIDS • AUDITORY TRAINING • DISCIPLINE
HOW TO TRAIN YOUR CHILD • SPEECH READING
WHAT TO EXPECT FROM YOUR CHILD • SCHOOLS

Although this book is written for the laymen, it is expected that many *physicians and other professional people might find it useful.* Futhermore, it is the intention that the book will be suggested to parents by physicians, educators, psychologists, social workers, and others who come in contact with children having extensive hearing losses. *SPECIAL FEATURE:* The book includes a directory of schools for the deaf and hard of hearing in the United States and Canada.

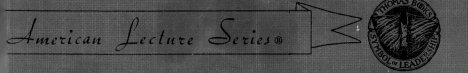

American Lecture Series ®

Your Deaf Child

❧ A GUIDE FOR PARENTS ❧

Publication Number 94
AMERICAN LECTURE SERIES

A Monograph in
AMERICAN LECTURES IN OTOLARYNGOLOGY

Edited by
NORTON CANFIELD, M.D.
Associate Professor of Otolaryngology
Yale University School of Medicine
New Haven, Connecticut

Your Deaf Child

❧ A GUIDE FOR PARENTS ❧

(SIXTH PRINTING)

By

HELMER R. MYKLEBUST

Professor of Audiology
Northwestern University

With a foreword by
HALLOWELL DAVIS, M.D.

CHARLES C THOMAS · PUBLISHER
Springfield · Illinois · U.S.A.

CHARLES C THOMAS • PUBLISHER
Bannerstone House
301-327 East Lawrence Avenue, Springfield, Illinois

Copyright, 1950, by

CHARLES C THOMAS • PUBLISHER

ISBN 0-398-03127-4 (paper)

First Edition, First Printing, October, 1950
First Edition, Second Printing, September, 1954
First Edition, Third Printing, January, 1960
First Edition, Fourth Printing, June, 1966
First Edition, Fifth Printing, January, 1970
First Edition, Sixth Printing, June, 1974

Printed in the United States of America
R

to
Bertha and Joe

FOREWORD

*I*t is not easy to bring up a child. Any parent, educator, or doctor will agree to this. I do not refer merely to providing the material necessities of food, clothing, and shelter, although these may present very real difficulties of their own. I refer to what is often called "training," but what is better called "social education." Every child must learn to live with and get along with himself, his parents, his brothers and sisters, his playmates, his teachers, and finally the whole world. Habits and emotional attitudes formed in early years may influence his behavior, his self-confidence, his sense of security, and what is summed up as his "social adjustment" throughout his whole life.

Some wisdom in guiding and training children is gained by parents through experience, even without help or advice from others, but then it is too late to go back and correct the mistakes that were made in the learning. Parents, particularly parents faced with the new problems of a first child, rightly look to the experience of others to acquaint them with the problems they must face and to help them avoid the pitfalls of ignorance. Many excellent books have been written to help parents in this way, and some of them have rightly gained the popularity of "best sellers." As the problems of modern life become more and more complicated, the task of adjusting to them becomes more and more difficult. Therefore, even for the parents themselves, such books become more and more important.

With so-called normal children we do not start entirely in the dark, books or no books. At least we were once more or less normal children ourselves, we have known other normal children and we have talked with their parents. But with the child who is handicapped by deafness it is different as well as more difficult. How many parents of deaf children were deaf children themselves? How many have previously known other deaf children and talked with their parents about the special problems of the deaf? And yet, when the misfortune of deafness strikes a child, either at birth or later, the parents have all of the usual problems of training a child in addition to the very special problems of deafness.

Parents of deaf children need to know about these special problems, and expert advice is essential. We all take our own hearing so much for granted that it requires a very special effort of the imagination to realize what it is like to be deaf. Even stopping up our ears does not tell us. Enough sound comes through so that we can still get along pretty well if people will only speak up. We are only mildly hard of hearing, and still have no idea what it is like to be really deaf.

Fortunately severe loss of hearing in children is rather rare. Consequently only a small number of teachers specialize in this work and are really fully aware of the problems. Perhaps they have learned to think in terms of a world without ears, which is the world of the deaf child. It is to these teachers with special experience that parents of deaf children must turn for information as to the difficulties of their deaf child. To them also parents must turn for help with their own special difficulties, their special responsibilities in training, in educating, and in "bringing up" a deaf child.

Deaf children *can* be brought up successfully. Deaf children can and do, with proper help and special training, grow up to be fully responsible, self-supporting, well-adjusted, and happy adults. But all of this does not happen by itself or by chance. The parents must make a special effort, and they must be able to get the information they need.

Dr. Myklebust, one of the expert teachers of the deaf in the United States, writes his book for the parents of deaf children. It is for parents who are asking for information and who want to do the best possible for their deaf child. He is a technical expert himself but he writes for the average, everyday parent; not just for parents with a college education but for all parents of deaf children. He puts important ideas in simple, direct language. Many of the things he writes may seem simple and obvious because deaf children have the same familiar problems as other children; but deaf children have one big special handicap in addition. Dr. Myklebust explains this handicap and then goes through familiar situations in bringing up children and shows what new forms the familiar situations take for deaf children. He tells what to do about them, and tells it clearly and simply. He answers for all who can read the questions that have been put to him over and over again by dozens and dozens of parents of deaf children whom he has taught.

Few books of this sort have been written. Most writing about the education and training of deaf children has been written by teachers for other teachers or by specialists for other specialists. This book is for parents. It will open the eyes of many to the happy possibilities that lie ahead for deaf children, if parents really understand their child's problems and if they will deal with them according to Dr. Myklebust's sound advice.

HALLOWELL DAVIS, M.D.

Central Institute for the Deaf
St. Louis, Missouri

PREFACE

Over a period of years progress has been made in the prevention and management of deafness. Many different types of specialists now are working directly with deaf and hard of hearing children; advancements continue to be made on all fronts. One of the outstanding advances is the recognition that no one is of more importance to the child with a hearing loss than his parents. Parents know that they can and should be of direct help to their child. As a result they are now organizing parents' clubs all over the nation. They want to help each other and to join with professional workers in the battle against deafness.

This book is written for parents. It has grown out of a number of years of association with deaf and hard of hearing children and their parents. It has been written mainly at the request of many parents who felt that it would be helpful to have a guide to the challenging task that lay before them. If this book serves this purpose well, I will feel that I have in small measure repaid the many parents who through their patience, tolerance, sympathy, and understanding have taught me so much. To them I am and continue to be greatly indebted.

Many of my colleagues, assistants, and students have contributed to this book through their interest, cooperation, and stimulation. I acknowledge my obligation to the staff of the New

Jersey School for the Deaf where I first became especially interested in working with parents. Invaluable criticism of the manuscript has been given by Miss Josephine Timberlake, Executive Secretary of the Volta Bureau; Dr. Powrie Doctor, Professor of English and History at Gallaudet College and Editor of the *American Annals of the Deaf;* Dr. Hallowell Davis, Director of Research at the Central Institute for the Deaf; Dr. Raymond Carhart, Professor of Audiology at Northwestern University; and by the Editor, Dr. Norton Canfield of the Yale University School of Medicine. To them all I express my gratitude. I am also grateful to Milton Brutten, my clinical assistant, for his painstaking help in the final preparation of the manuscript, to Miss Judy Pierce for her patience and perseverance in doing the drawings, and to Miss Donna Weckler for her careful and diligent typing of the manuscript. Finally I am indebted to my wife, not only for her assistance with the manuscript, but for her unfailing confidence and encouragement.

HELMER R. MYKLEBUST

Evanston, Illinois

CONTENTS

Foreword *by Hallowell Davis, M.D.* vii

Preface xi

Chapter I

WHAT DEAFNESS MEANS TO YOU 1

Deafness—Past and Present 4

The Ear and How We Hear 6

What Sound Means 7

When a Child Is Deaf 9

Your Child Is Deaf 11

Chapter II

CAUSES AND TYPES OF DEAFNESS 14

Age of Becoming Deaf 16

Importance of Cause 18

Types of Deafness 20

Children Deaf from Meningitis 23

Children with Multiple Handicaps 24

The Number of Children with Impaired Hearing . . . 25

Chapter III

YOUR ATTITUDES AND WHAT THEY MEAN 26

Attitude of Acceptance 28

Attitude of Overprotection 29

Contents

The Wishful Attitude 30
Attitude of Indifference 31

Chapter IV

THE DEAF CHILD AND HIS NEEDS 34
Need for Consistency 35
Need for Being a Part of the Family 38
Need for Success 40
Need for Activity 42
Need for Independence 45
Health Needs 47
Need for Expression 48

Chapter V

LEARNING TO CARE FOR HIMSELF 51
Learning to Eat 55
Toilet Training 59
Discipline and Punishment 60
Jealousy 63
Fears 65
Temper Tantrums, Quarreling, and Stubbornness . . . 66
Nailbiting and Thumbsucking 68
Walking 69
Noisy Breathing and Vocalizing 69
Sleep and Rest 70
Neighbors and Playmates 71

Chapter VI

LEARNING TO COMMUNICATE 73
Your Concern about Speech 74
Their Abilities Vary 75
Some Have Residual Hearing 76
Tests of Hearing 77
The Use of Hearing Aids 79
Speech Reading 81
The Child Who Has No Hearing 83
Auditory Training 85

Contents

The Child Who Loses His Hearing 88
Overcoming the Problem of Communication 89
Going to School 89

Chapter VII

WHAT TO EXPECT FROM YOUR CHILD 93
Deaf Children Are Normal Mentally 94
Deafness and Personality 95
Deafness and School Achievement 95
Earning a Living 96
A Hearing World 97
Helping Other Parents 99

Chapter VIII

ORGANIZATIONS WHICH CAN HELP—READING MATERIALS—DIRECTORY OF SCHOOLS 102

Part One

ORGANIZATIONS WHICH ARE PARTICULARLY INTERESTED IN PROVIDING INFORMATION TO PARENTS OF DEAF AND HARD OF HEARING CHILDREN 103

Part Two

BOOKS AND PERIODICALS WHICH ARE ESPECIALLY HELPFUL TO PARENTS OF DEAF AND HARD OF HEARING CHILDREN . . . 109

Part Three

SCHOOLS FOR THE DEAF AND THE HARD OF HEARING IN THE UNITED STATES AND CANADA 115

INDEX 131

Your Deaf Child
A GUIDE FOR PARENTS

Chapter 1

WHAT DEAFNESS MEANS TO YOU

*E*veryone who has a hearing loss is commonly referred to as being deaf. Usually these people are not deaf; they are hard of hearing. They have lost some of their hearing, but they still have a considerable amount of residual hearing. Residual hearing is the amount of hearing that remains after some of it has been lost. The hard of hearing can hear sounds if they are made louder. They have hearing which is usable. For this reason these people are rightly called hard of hearing. Persons whose hearing loss is so great that their hearing is of no use to them are called deaf. Making sounds louder is of no help to them. They cannot hear speech under any circumstances.

This book is written for you parents who have a child with a loss of hearing which is so great that it has prevented him from learning to talk as he should. He may have usable residual hearing but, because he cannot hear everyday conversation, he has not learned to talk. The fact that he is not able to hear everyday speech does not mean that he is deaf. He may have usable hearing. If so, he will be able to hear sounds if they are made

I

louder. This is done through the use of a hearing aid. Perhaps your child has no hearing. He would then rightly be called deaf. Making sounds louder would not help him.

As you read this book, remember the differences between children who are deaf and those who are hard of hearing. However, this book is written for you parents whose children have

not learned to talk because they do not hear well enough to hear everyday speech. The term **deaf** will be used in this book to include all of these children. Deafness is used to mean all degrees of hearing loss. The loss may be only to the extent of preventing your child from hearing speech, or it may be a total loss for all sounds. Likewise, the terms **impaired hearing** and **hearing loss** will be used for all children who do not hear well enough to learn to talk without some help.

There is much that you can and should do for your child during his preschool years. To be of the most help to him, you must accept as a challenge the problem which he presents. In general, you will be inclined to think too much about his deafness and not enough about his growing and developing normally. Your child is like any normal child in most ways. He is different from them mainly because he has not learned to talk at the usual age. Naturally, this means he cannot make *you* understand easily and you find it difficult to make *him* understand. There is much you can do to teach him and to train him in every way during these important early years of his life. During these early years, your child will develop habits and patterns which will be important to him throughout his life.

You will need assistance with your deaf child from time to time, but no one can do for him what you can. You have a special responsibility toward him which only you can fulfill. The greatest contribution you can make to his future is to realize that with your assistance he will be a happy child and a self-reliant citizen.

The job ahead of you is not an easy one. There are many things that you must learn and do in order to give your child the training he needs. You may use this book as a guide for your program. In Chapter I you will find a discussion of how the deaf were treated in early times, how we hear, the difficulties of determining deafness in children, and what your responsibilities are as the parents of a child who has a hearing loss. Chapter II is a consideration of the causes and the different types of deafness, and the difference between children who are born deaf and those who become deaf after they have learned to speak. The importance of your attitudes is stressed in Chapter III. Four common attitudes are discussed: the attitudes of acceptance, overprotection, wishfulness, and indifference. Your deaf child's particular needs are discussed in Chapter IV: his need for consistency, for being a part of the family, for success, for activity, for independence, and for expression.

3

In Chapter V you will find suggestions for training your child to care for himself; learning to eat, toilet habits, discipline, jealousy, fears, and temper tantrums are some of the training problems considered. How you can help your child to learn to communicate is discussed in Chapter VI: the use of residual hearing, learning to talk without the help of hearing, and learning speech reading. Chapter VII is a consideration of what you can expect from your child as he grows up. You will find suggestions in this book easier to follow if you read it from the beginning to the end without skipping chapters.

DEAFNESS—PAST AND PRESENT

Deafness has been known to exist since the beginning of recorded history. The treatment of deaf people during those early days of history was very different from what it is now. They were thought to be stupid and considered to be possessed of evil spirits. They were denied the usual rights and privileges of other citizens. Their families often did not want them because deafness was feared and thought to be an evil omen.

Being aware of this early attitude toward the deaf helps us to understand certain opinions regarding them which are common even today. Often the uninformed still think of them as being odd and queer. We find individuals who confuse deafness with low mental ability and who consider the deaf unable to fulfill their obligations as citizens. In daily life people often are surprised to learn that the deaf are happy, socially capable, and self-supporting. Another popular misconception is that deaf people are all alike. Of course this is not true. They are as different one from another as are any other group of individuals.

In spite of their treatment in early times and in spite of present day misconceptions, the deaf have made a place for themselves in society. They have a heritage which is an inspiration to all who are familiar with it. These people ask only to be given an opportunity to learn and to demonstrate their abilities. But,

4

in order for you to be a wise and patient parent, you must understand that there is confusion on the part of many people concerning the deaf. Only by being aware of this confusion can you fully appreciate the problem which faces your child.

Naturally we are fearful and disturbed when we first experience deafness in our own family. As a parent of a little deaf child, you must recognize without resentment that people with deafness are a small group as compared to those with normal hearing. Also, misconceptions concerning them will continue. You parents must realize that it is only in recent years that science has studied the problem of deafness with any great vigor. Not until the past quarter century was deafness studied seriously by scientists. During this time we have learned a great deal about deafness and about the deaf. As yet this information is not easy for you to obtain and it is not common knowledge to the population in general.

During the recent war, various branches of the military services were required to study and rehabilitate the veterans who had lost their hearing. As a result of this program, there has been a tremendous increase in the scientific study of the problems relating to hearing impairment. There are now many hearing clinics throughout the country and more are being organized. These clinics are similar to those established during the war. Often several specialists, such as physicians, speech correctionists, and psychologists work together in the examination of a particular individual with a hearing loss. A new term is now used which unites these specialties. This term is **Audiology** and it means the science of hearing. Because of this new science of hearing we are learning more about the medical treatment of hearing loss, the use of hearing aids by both children and adults, and more about the teaching of speech and speech reading. While much remains to be learned, we now know more about what a hearing loss means to your child and what you can do to understand and train him better.

THE EAR AND HOW WE HEAR

The ear is the organ of hearing. For purposes of discussion and study it may be divided into three parts: the outer ear, the middle ear, and the inner ear. The part which is visible on the side of the head (the pinna) and the opening (the auditory canal) is referred to as the outer ear. The outer ear "collects" and "directs" sound vibrations into the hearing mechanism. Often if

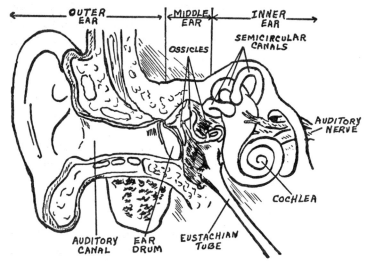

we have difficulty in hearing, we "cup" our hand over our ear. This helps the outer ear collect and direct sound so that we can hear better. The outer ear also serves as a protection for the middle ear and the inner ear.

At the inner end of the auditory canal is the eardrum (tympanic membrane). This is the beginning of the middle ear. In the middle ear are three small bones, known as the ossicles. These bones commonly are referred to individually as the hammer (malleus), the anvil (incus), and the stirrup (stapes) because of their shapes. The ossicles form a chain from the eardrum to the inner ear. When sound waves strike the eardrum, it vibrates and sets the ossicles in motion. In this way the middle ear is a conductive mechanism which transmits or carries the sound from the outer ear to the inner ear. Also, in the middle ear is an opening known as the eustachian tube, which connects with the nasal cavity. This tube or opening provides ventilation for the middle ear and also provides equal air pressure on both sides of the eardrum.

The inner ear is a chamber filled with fluid. Within this chamber is a snail-shaped tube known as the cochlea. The cochlea is the vital organ of hearing. It changes the sound vibrations from the middle ear into electrical impulses which travel as sound messages to the brain. Also, within the inner ear are the semicircular canals. These canals are closely connected with the cochlea, but they do not serve the purpose of hearing. Rather, they give us a sense of balance. The close connection between our senses of balance and hearing is revealed in some types of deafness where the disease causing deafness also affects balance. This is discussed more fully in Chapter II.

WHAT SOUND MEANS

When you bring your child to the doctor for a hearing test, he finds the faintest sound that your child can hear. This is to determine your child's hearing acuity. A full discussion of hearing tests is reserved for Chapter VI. We shall now consider some of the aspects of sound itself.

When a solid object is struck and is caused to vibrate, it in turn sets the air in motion. When these air vibrations reach our ears, we have a sensation of hearing and we refer to what we hear as sound. Sound is sometimes described as air-carried vibrations. A good example of vibrations producing sound is that of the violin. The bow is drawn across the strings of the violin causing them to vibrate. These vibrations of the strings make the surrounding air vibrate, and in this way these vibrations are carried to our ears.

Sounds as we know them are not all alike. A sound can be weak or strong, soft or loud. The loudness depends on what the scientist calls intensity, or sound energy. In the testing of hearing, the energy of sound is measured in decibels. The decibel often is called the unit of measure of sound much as a foot or a yard are units of measure of length. However, the decibel is not a fixed unit, but rather it is a ratio between the energies of two sounds.

As a sound travels through the air, it can vibrate very fast or it can vibrate slowly. The rate at which any sound vibrates is called the frequency of the sound. It means the number of complete double vibrations that the sound makes in one second. Frequency is what we know as pitch. When the scientist calls a sound a high-frequency sound, he means it is vibrating several thousand times in one second. When we hear such a sound, we call it a high-pitch sound. Low-frequency sounds are what we call low-pitch sounds. Human beings can hear sounds which vary in frequency from 20 to 20,000 double vibrations in one second. (Middle C on the musical scale is 256 double vibrations per second.) Some animals, such as dogs, have a much wider range of hearing than we have.

Most everyday sounds are made up of a mixture of many frequencies. Speech and music are examples of sounds which consist of a combination of many high and low-frequency sounds. This mixture or combination of sound frequencies determines the quality of sound. We learn to recognize voices by their particular quality. If a sound consists of only one frequency, it is called a pure tone. Such sounds are not complex and in quality are very different from the sounds such as speech and music. Pure tones often are used in testing hearing.

It is not necessary for you to know the technical aspects of sound. It is to your advantage, however, to know a few of the fundamentals of sound. For example, if you know what sound is, how everyday sounds differ from each other, and how sounds can be made louder, you can understand better the total problem of your child's hearing loss. You will be especially interested in these fundamentals of sound if your child can profit from using a hearing aid.

WHEN A CHILD IS DEAF

It is rarely possible to know simply by looking at the ear whether or not a child has a hearing loss. In addition to examining his ears, often it is necessary to study the whole child and to compare his total behavior with the known characteristics of children having hearing difficulties.

The doctor who examines your child knows that some children who seem not to hear well are not really deaf or even hard of hearing. He knows that some children appear to have a hearing loss when their real problem is psychological. These children, because of insecurity, jealousy, over-indulgence by their parents, and for many other reasons, feel that they can get along more easily by not hearing and speaking. It is not that they want to be deaf. Rather the circumstances are such that they find it more in accordance with their needs not to respond when spoken to and not to speak themselves. Not many children develop this type of psychological problem, but some do and they are sometimes confused with those who have real hearing difficulties. The specialist is always on the lookout for these children.

When you take your child to the doctor for examination, he will observe whether your child appears to be like still another group of children who seem not to hear when they too have normal hearing. These children can hear but are unable to *understand* what they hear. Because of an injury to the brain (often occurring at birth) they cannot interpret the sounds which they hear as well as the normal child does. This condition is known as aphasia. Some aphasic children, apparently because they hear sound constantly and because it has no meaning to them, learn to disregard sound; they ignore sound completely.

9

They become so skillful in ignoring all sounds that they appear to have no hearing. Again, the specialist is able to compare these children with the known characteristics of children who have deafness in a true sense. He is able to determine by a study of the whole child whether or not your child has a true hearing loss.

At times it is necessary to determine whether a child is appearing not to hear and is not speaking because he is mentally retarded, rather than because he is deaf. Likewise, a child who has a real difficulty of hearing might wrongly be considered mentally retarded. If you have questions regarding your child's mental ability, you should seek the advice of a specialist who can examine your child psychologically. Many universities now have clinics where such advice can be secured.

It is possible that your child has only a slight loss of hearing. On the other hand, he may have a moderate loss, a profound or a complete loss of hearing. Usually it is easier to know that there is a loss of hearing when the loss is great, rather than when the loss is mild. For example, your child may hear certain sounds normally but actually have a serious loss of hearing for those sounds which he must hear in order to learn to speak. If so, he will hear many noises, such as the clapping of hands or the snapping of fingers, and he will be thought to have normal hearing. Frequently these children have been confused with the mentally retarded or the aphasic. It is difficult in infancy to pick out these children, but to confuse them with other types of handicapped children is extremely unfortunate. When a child has been confused in this way, he may become difficult to handle and may develop serious adjustment difficulties. Fortunately new ways of testing and examining children now make it possible to determine at an early age the type and the degree of the hearing loss.

You must realize that your child may have a serious loss of hearing, even though he hears the door close or looks around when the dog barks and when you clap your hands. The specialist, who understands the various types of hearing losses, knows that in this case your child hears some sounds well but does not hear the main sounds needed to hear speech.

You, as parents of a deaf child, know that there are ways in which your child differs from the child with normal hearing. You know that he does not hear the everyday sounds in your household. He does not hear you when you call him. He does not hear the telephone or the doorbell. He may hear a loud sound, such as an automobile horn. He does not learn to talk at the usual age because he cannot hear you speak and he cannot imitate what you say. Perhaps you have noticed that he relies on his eyes to get information. This dependence on his eyes causes him to watch all kinds of movement. He is always looking at something and changing his position so that he can *see* what is happening. It is no wonder that he is always "on the go." Because he wants to see, he is much more at a loss in even moderate darkness than is the child with normal hearing. He learns to use his voice to call to you, but his voice does not have the usual quality of the hearing child's. You may have noticed too that he shuffles and drags his feet when he walks.

These are some of the characteristics of the deaf child. They will be discussed more fully throughout the book.

YOUR CHILD IS DEAF

When you first learned that your child was deaf, perhaps like many other parents you were stunned and bewildered. You may have felt great sorrow, shame, remorse, and even resentment. "Why my child?" may have kept running through your mind. You had plans and aspirations for your child but when you learned about his deafness, these plans and hopes were shattered. You could think of nothing but his deafness. Maybe it was your first child; maybe your second or third. If it was your first child there probably was a special desperation which can come only with the first little one.

Perhaps only you parents who have gone through the experience of being informed that your child is deaf, and have lived through those hectic, bewildering months that follow, can actually understand and appreciate what it means. The feeling of loneliness, disillusionment, despair, and anxiousness seems to

be almost unbearable. These feelings often are so intense and persist for so long a time that they cause you to be a greater problem than your child. These feelings may prevent you from believing that your child is deaf. As a result, you "inquire" from specialist after specialist in the often unconscious hope that you will find someone who will say that your child is not deaf. This is an unfortunate experience for both you and your child. You often weep in his presence and look at him with a depressed, sorrowful expression. This is one reason that we often see deaf children who rarely smile and who appear sad and unhappy.

It is natural when you learn that your child is deaf, that you go through a period of great unhappiness. *But this period must end as soon as possible.* You must begin making new plans for your child. You must realize that you are not alone with your problem. You must also realize that it is your responsibility as a parent of a deaf child to show him that life has purpose, hope and meaning; that you can accept this challenge and proceed to work out new plans which take into consideration your child's deafness.

You must remember that nothing is more important to your child than his family. It is from his family that he first learns to "give and take." During these early preschool years you as a family are laying the pattern of his personality. *Your deaf child will give to life and in return expect from it according to the pattern you set for him.* For example, if you feel that life has been unjust, that you have had more than your share of misfortune and trouble, then your child will assume an attitude of self-pity as he becomes older. He may feel that life has treated him unfairly. On the other hand, if you feel that all people have their share of trouble, that all children are different, that your child, although he is deaf, can be like other children in most respects, then he is learning a great deal from you. He is learning that deafness presents certain limitations which he must accept, but that other children also have their problems. Perhaps some other child's problem is even greater than his.

Chapter II

CAUSES AND TYPES OF DEAFNESS

A mother and father had noticed for several months that their two-year-old son did not pay attention when they talked to him or when they rang a bell behind him. They also noticed that he was not awakened by loud sounds. These parents had had no experience with deafness. They did not fully realize what was ahead of them when they first took their child to the doctor. However, they knew they should consult someone who could tell them why their child was not learning to talk and why he did not seem to notice sounds. After examining their child, the doctor told them that he was deaf. Although they had suspected deafness this information was a staggering blow to them. They asked how this could be, why their little Jimmy was deaf, what caused his not being able to hear, whether he could be made to hear. Perhaps many of you have had this same experience. Perhaps you have asked these same questions.

Because of the rapid scientific advancement in medicine and in other professional specialties in recent years, we have become more aware of what causes deafness. Parents are asking more questions about the causes and about the types of deafness. This is as it should be. There are many different causes of impaired hearing. The ear is a complex organ and can be affected in many different ways. How the ear has been affected determines the type of hearing loss which has resulted. You will understand

your child better when you become familiar with the causes and types of deafness.

Most people think that hearing impairments are all alike. In some ways your child's hearing loss may be like that of others. You should not conclude, however, that his hearing loss is the same as that of his uncle, cousin, or grandfather without first learning what type of hearing loss he has. Neither should you conclude, without asking your doctor, that his deafness is like that of a friend's child. The type of deafness which your child has may not be the same as that of someone you know. You should not compare your child's condition with that of others and come to conclusions without the help of a specialist. Often parents, because of the influence of relatives and friends, do not try to find the cause and the type of their child's deafness. Therefore, treatments which might be helpful are not given. On the other hand there are friends and relatives who urge further examinations after the cause and the type have been determined. You should continue to seek advice as long as there is a possibility that something can be done to improve your child's hearing. However, it is equally important after you have been told that medical treatments will not help your child, that you not continue to seek cures which do not exist.

AGE OF BECOMING DEAF

In addition to the cause and type of deafness, the age at which your child lost his hearing is important in your understanding of what it means to him. If he became deaf after he had learned to talk, he may remember much of his speech. We know, however, that children who lose their hearing after they have learned to talk do lose much of their speech in a few months unless they are given help. Your child should have speech training immediately after losing his hearing. This is discussed more completely in Chapter VI. We are concerned here with the fact that if your child had learned to talk before he lost his hearing, he has an advantage in speech and in his general use of language.

If your child has never heard or if he lost his hearing before learning to talk, it will be more difficult for him to learn to speak and to communicate in other ways. He has no language background on which to build. He has no understanding of sound. He does not know that things have names and that sounds have meanings. You must remember that it is natural for us to speak the way we hear. We imitate the speech sounds around us. If we grow up in the southern states, we speak with a "southern accent." If we grow up in the middle west, we speak with a "midwestern accent." Likewise, the child who hears inaccurately will speak inaccurately. He will speak the way he hears. For example, for "shoe" he may say "oo." He does not hear the "sh" sound so he does not pronounce it. If your child cannot hear any speech sounds, then he cannot imitate your speech and he does not learn to talk naturally. There is nothing wrong with his organs of speech. He simply does not hear, so he does not learn to use his speech organs and to produce the sounds which we call speech. Children who have never heard sound have more difficulty with language, speech and school work. However, because they do not miss hearing, as do children who once heard, they often have an advantage in fitting into their families and into society.

The little child who is now deaf but who had hearing for two, three, four years or more finds it very difficult to fit into a world without sounds. He goes through a period of feeling lost and shut off from you and his everyday surroundings. Often he cries easily and tries in other ways to show you that he feels lonely and sad. You must be very patient and sympathetic at this time. If you have patience and courage yourself you can help him to overcome these feelings gradually. Remember that when the lights are turned out at night he has no contact with you. Before losing his hearing he could hear the familiar sounds and voices in the next room. These familiar voices and noises assured him that everything was all right. Now because he cannot hear these sounds, he may be afraid and seem to be "so different," as many parents have said. During this time that he is learning to live without sound it is wise to use a night light. You should help him to overcome his fears in every way possible.

If your child has been deaf from birth he does not feel lost and shut off from you and the world in the same way as the child who at one time had hearing. He does not miss hearing because he has not learned to enjoy sound. Rather, through his association with you and other people who have normal hearing, he gradually becomes aware that he does not hear as you do. One of your most difficult problems is to make him feel that he is a real part of your family; he should not be made to feel different. The speech which the normal child understands even before he learns to talk himself is a strong bond which unites him with his parents and other members of his family. He learns to recognize voices and he is pleased when he hears them. His hearing keeps him in touch with his surroundings, although he may not be able to see what is happening. The child who has never heard does not feel this bond, which is formed by his being able to hear speech. He must be kept in contact with his family in other ways. This is discussed more fully in Chapter IV. You can to a great extent prevent him from feeling different from other children. You need not call attention to his deafness. He will learn that most people can hear. This fact need not be emphasized to him. The more he is treated as any other child, without calling attention to his deafness, the better it is for him.

You see from the fact that different problems are presented by the child who has never heard and the child who has had normal hearing before losing it that the age at which hearing was lost is of considerable importance. The age at which deafness occurred is called the age of onset. Knowing the age of onset helps you to know how to handle your child. Knowing the cause and type of hearing loss helps you to understand what can be done by medical treatment, by hearing aids, and by special methods of instruction.

IMPORTANCE OF CAUSE

As your child grows older, he will wonder about the cause of his hearing loss. One of the common questions of deaf children as they reach adolescence is, "What caused my deafness?" Most parents are concerned about the cause of their child's hearing loss. Often they wonder about having another child, fearing that he too may be deaf. Furthermore, they worry about the possibility of their child having deaf children when he grows up and marries. Several parents have stated that while they can accept the problem of their own child, they would be extremely regretful if he too should be faced with the same problem. Even though it is often hard to discover the cause you should do so whenever possible for your own satisfaction and for that of your child's. Better methods for the study of causes are being developed. As a result of this progress we know that in the past some children have been called deaf because of heredity when their hearing loss was due to other conditions occurring before birth, at the time of birth, or in very early infancy.

Hearing losses can be classified into groups on the basis of cause. The scientific study and explanation of causes is called **etiology.** When children are grouped according to the cause of their impairment, they are said to be classified etiologically. In the past the terms "congenital" and "acquired" have been used for this purpose. Because these terms present certain confusions scientifically we have substituted the terms **endogenous** and **exogenous.** An endogenous hearing loss means that it is due to hereditary causes. An exogenous hearing loss is due to accident or disease occurring at any time before or after birth; it is due to causes which are not hereditary. In each of these groups there are children with different degrees of hearing loss. The degree of loss may vary from a slight loss for certain sounds to a complete loss of hearing for all sounds. As was stated in Chapter I the degree of the hearing loss is the main difference between the deaf and the hard of hearing. Most hearing defects in childhood which are not endogenous are caused by meningitis, scarlet fever, ear infections, pneumonia, birth injury, whooping cough, and accidents which injure the ear.

In recent years physicians have found that a child may be born with a hearing loss if the mother had German measles during pregnancy, especially during the first three months. Because we have learned that German measles during pregnancy may cause deafness greater effort will be put forth to prevent expectant mothers from getting this disease. Some parents can now be told accurately why their child is deaf, because before we knew that German measles could cause deafness these parents were told that the cause was unknown; in some instances it was wrongly called hereditary.

TYPES OF DEAFNESS

Perhaps you have been told by a specialist that your child has **nerve deafness.** This type of hearing loss is common in infancy. Nerve deafness means that there is something wrong with the inner ear. This kind of hearing loss may be caused by a hereditary (endogenous) condition or by diseases (exogenous) such as meningitis, pneumonia, scarlet fever, and whooping cough. Accidents such as birth injury, skull fracture, and explosions may injure the inner ear and cause nerve deafness. There are of course many other diseases and accidents which may damage the inner ear.

Nerve deafness cannot be cured. There is no known treatment that will bring back or improve your child's hearing if he has a nerve type of hearing loss. This is true whether his loss was caused by disease or accident. Some parents find it hard to believe that their child cannot be made to hear. They seek and try many "cure-all" treatments. These treatments are never suggested or recommended by reputable ear doctors. Children who are taken from place to place and made to go through these unsound "cure-all" treatments usually develop other problems. One little deaf boy six years of age, whom we saw often, was taken by his parents to be "treated" for a nerve type of hearing loss once a week for a year. The person giving the treatments was well known for his practice of taking advantage of parents who would "try anything." Several physicians had told the parents that treatments would not help their child's hearing. After a number of "treatments" this little boy became such a problem in school that the parents were told it was impossible to have him with other children. He was destructive, extremely active, ate and slept poorly, and could not fit into or take part in any school activities. It was not the "treatments" alone which made this boy become so hard to handle; it was also that he felt his parents did not approve of him and that they were not pleased with him as he was. By insisting on these treatments his parents were really expressing a dissatisfaction with him. Children feel this dissatisfaction and try to overcome it. Often they refuse to obey. Sometimes they become very bashful and shy. There are many other ways in which children show their unhappiness because of the disappointment felt by their parents. When their child's hearing does not improve the parents' hopes are destroyed and the family tensions become even greater. Only harm can come from such useless attempts even though the intentions behind them are good.

Deafness caused by diseases which affect the middle ear is called **conduction deafness.** Conduction deafness means that there is something wrong with that part of the ear which conducts sound. We learned in Chapter I that the middle ear serves as the conductor of sound to the inner ear. The common cause of conduction deafness is infection and inflammation of the middle ear. This is called **otitis media** and is usually due to infection behind the ear drum, often occurring in children who have many head colds. Frequently there is a discharge of fluid from the ear. Children who have middle ear infections often complain of earaches. If your child has a discharge from the ear he should be under the care of an ear specialist. Often hearing can be helped by proper treatments. In recent years physicians have developed improved methods for treating middle ear infections. If there is a discharge from your child's ear, treatment should not be neglected. Continued discharge may mean that the ear is becoming more and more affected and that more and more hearing is being lost. If the hearing cannot be improved it is very important that you try to prevent it from becoming poorer.

Another common disease of the middle ear is **otosclerosis.** In this disease a bony substance grows around a part of the middle ear called the oval window. This growth prevents the little bones in the middle ear from moving freely and from carrying the

sound easily to the inner ear. This type of hearing loss rarely occurs in children. Usually it occurs between 20 and 30 years of age. A recently developed operation, called the fenestration operation, is now commonly performed for this condition. Because otosclerosis is so rare in children this operation, which has proved so helpful to many adults, unfortunately is seldom of help to deaf children. There are a few cases, however, where a child has been known to have otosclerosis from birth. The fenestration operation has been helpful with these children.

CHILDREN DEAF FROM MENINGITIS

If your child is deaf because he has had meningitis he will be somewhat different from children whose deafness was not caused by meningitis. Meningitis children, as they are often called, usually have poor balance. The disease not only destroys the hearing mechanism in the inner ear but it also frequently destroys the semicircular canals, which give us our sense of balance. So the meningitis child, when he is first permitted to be active, finds it difficult to walk even though he may have been able to walk well before he had the disease. At first, he may stagger and run or walk with a "lunging gait." You as a parent may have been greatly concerned about his poor balance. Sometimes, during the first several months following the illness, the falling, stumbling, and lunging which the child experiences is a greater problem than his deafness. This is a difficult time for the child as well as his parents. Above all you should not be fearful and anxious about his poor balance. If you are, your child will become fearful and he will not try his best to overcome his lack of balance. It is better to help and to encourage him as he again gains control and learns to balance himself, just as he did when he took his first step. He will learn to use his eyes to help him keep his balance. Through practice and the regaining of his strength he again learns to walk and to run. Usually within a year he will regain good balance. Many boys whose deafness was caused by meningitis have become good athletes.

As soon as your child is old enough, he should be told about his condition in a straightforward and sympathetic way. It is especially important to tell him that he will have some difficulty in maintaining good balance in the dark. This is because he has learned to depend a great deal on his eyes for keeping his balance. We know from experience with many children deaf from meningitis that with wise guidance and training they will develop into happy and successful adults. Like other nerve types

23

of hearing loss, deafness caused by meningitis cannot be cured. The inner ear has been damaged and it cannot be made to recover.

CHILDREN WITH MULTIPLE HANDICAPS

Children who have more than one handicap are called the **multiple handicapped** children. During recent years a great deal of study has been given to such children. We know that some individuals with two or more handicaps often take their places as happy, independent members of society. The problem of schooling and training, however, is more difficult. For example, most schools for children with impaired hearing do not have facilities for children who are both deaf and seriously crippled. Neither do most schools for the crippled have a program for deaf children. Most special schools do not provide for deaf children who are also seriously mentally retarded, or who have poor eyesight.

One reason that most schools for handicapped children do not have programs for the multiple handicapped is that the type of program which is most suitable for them has not been developed. But much progress has been made in recent years. Better methods of examination and training are being developed constantly. In order for any particular child to have his best opportunity he should be placed for education and training with those children that he is most like. Another way of stating this is that he should be handled mainly on the basis of his major handicap. This means that even though your child is deaf, if he is also seriously crippled (unable to walk, etc.) he will profit most from being in a school for crippled children even though most of the children in such a school have normal hearing. If your child is seriously mentally retarded, he will profit most from being in a program for children with mental handicaps. The deafness must not be ignored; it simply should be considered secondary to a handicap which is more urgent. Fortunately many schools for the crippled, schools for the mentally retarded, and others, are now getting teachers who have specialized in working with children who have impaired hearing. If your child has a multiple handicap you can do much for him and for other children like him by encouraging such programs.

If your child has a handicap in addition to deafness you have a more difficult task before you than if his only handicap were that of hearing. You should consider all of his limitations but also you must emphasize his best abilities.

THE NUMBER OF CHILDREN WITH IMPAIRED HEARING

Most authorities agree that between one and two percent of all children have a hearing loss which is so great that they may be considered deaf. During the year 1949, there were 18,843 children in schools for the deaf in the United States.* There are more deaf children of school age than this figure indicates, because we know that not all deaf children are in these special schools. However, the total number of deaf people, children and adults, is small. This is one reason that the general public is so poorly informed about deafness and about deaf people. Most people simply have never encountered the problem of deafness in children. There are a great many more children who are hard of hearing than there are children who are deaf. Including both the hard of hearing and the deaf, authorities state that there are between one and a half and two million children with impaired hearing in the United States. It is well to remember that even when these two groups are combined, they are a small number when compared to children with normal hearing. It will be necessary for you to explain your child's deafness to many of your friends and neighbors who are only vaguely aware of the nature of deafness in children.

American Annals of the Deaf, January, 1949.

Chapter III

YOUR ATTITUDES AND WHAT THEY MEAN

N othing is more important to your child than the feelings and attitudes which you express toward him. All parents at times are confused by their feelings; they know that "spoiling" their child may cause him to have serious problems in later life, but still they continue to indulge him. This is a common experience of parents of deaf children. It is not easy to understand the meaning of your attitudes and to prevent confusion of yourself and your child. It is not easy under ordinary circumstances and it becomes more difficult when you have a deaf child.

Perhaps you, like many parents, think it is only what you *do* for your child and what you *say* to him that really matters. Of course what you do and say are an important part of the way in which you handle your child. These are not only the important ways in which you influence him, however. Your feelings, such as annoyance, impatience, anger, fear, anxiety, despair, and sadness, or feelings of tolerance, patience, love, calmness, frankness, honesty, and happiness are as important to your child as what you *do* and *say*. This is especially true of a deaf child. He cannot get meanings from words as well as does the hearing child. He notices and responds more directly to your moods and attitudes. An example of this is the mother who came to us to discuss her daughter, Anne. Anne had considerable hearing but had not yet learned to talk. She was willful, persistent, independent, and demanding. She was a very capable little girl in most respects. Her mother realized that Anne was out of hand. She no longer responded to discipline; she was disobedient and very hard to manage. The mother told Anne that she loved her very much, *but Anne did not feel this love*. The mother was impatient when she helped Anne with dressing. When she explained to Anne that she should stay in the play yard she showed much fear and annoyance. In other words, Anne through her daily routine with her mother did not respond to her mother's statements that she loved her, but rather she was most influenced by the impatience, tension and lack of happiness which was being directly expressed by her mother. Of course, Anne's mother did not know she was showing her feelings. You, like Anne's mother, are constantly revealing your deeper feelings by the way you look at your child, the way you approach him, the way you help him with eating, dressing, and going to bed, as well as in many other ways. Your deaf child is constantly sensing your feelings. He knows when you are tense and unhappy, just as he knows when you are calm and happy. This is why nothing is more important to him than the feelings and attitudes with which his family surrounds him. These subtleties, because of their importance, must be understood and directed.

Many parents of deaf children have common questions concerning their attitudes. One of these questions is related to whether the deafness comes from the father's or mother's family. If the child has been deaf from birth or early infancy, and if the cause has not been determined, the parents immediately trace each other's family tree. Up to this time neither parent has given any real thought to the family tree of the other. Now suddenly it has become important and an issue. Many parents approach this issue calmly and sympathetically. Others blame and criticize each other. If the father finds that the mother has an uncle who had a hearing loss in later life he might assume an attitude of blame and fault-finding toward his wife, even though there may be no connection between the uncle's loss of hearing and their child's. The mother naturally tries to overcome this feeling of "weakness" in her family. So she "showers" the child with everything he wants. He is over-indulged. Or she may find it impossible to give the child sufficient love and understanding because he constantly reminds her of the "weakness" in her family. This is an illustration of the ways in which your attitudes can be damaging and perhaps be a greater handicap to your child than his deafness. One of the important needs of your child is that you have wholesome attitudes toward him.

ATTITUDE OF ACCEPTANCE

Parents express many different attitudes toward their deaf children. We have discussed these attitudes with a great many parents and find that in general they fall into four groups. The first group consists of those who have an attitude of wholesome acceptance. This means that you accept your child and that you are realistic about his handicap. You do not pretend that there are no problems or that you have never been bewildered and confused by these problems. You have acquired a calm, patient, sympathetic understanding. You are sure that you can solve all problems that will be encountered. You have a deep, profound love for your deaf child which is just like that felt by all parents who have an unusually good relationship with their children. This attitude of wholesome acceptance is the most difficult to develop. Usually it takes time and effort. Those of you who fall into this group can help other parents who have not acquired this attitude.

Recently a young mother of a deaf child was in the presence of an elderly woman who was the mother of a deaf son. The elderly woman's son had been educated in a school for the deaf and was now a successful painting contractor. The young mother was rebellious and confused. The elderly woman, through discussions with her, was able to help her a great deal.

Discussions of this type are helpful in the development of good attitudes and real appreciation of your child's needs.

ATTITUDE OF OVERPROTECTION

The second attitude which is common to many of you is one resulting in overprotection. This means that you protect your child from everyday situations and experiences which he needs to undergo in order to grow up and to become normally self-sufficient. You feel that because of his deafness he should not be expected to assume responsibility for himself. You do not teach him to dress and to feed himself at the usual age at which these habits are learned. Instead, you carefully look after all of his needs and help him with activities which he should learn to do for himself.

Through your attitude of overprotection your child gradually learns to expect people to wait on him. Later, as he grows older, he feels that society owes him everything. Such attitudes can be a greater handicap to your child than his deafness. If you have the feeling that you must protect your child from the everyday problems of living you should try to determine the reasons for feeling as you do. It may come from feelings of shame, embarrassment, and resentment. In trying to cover up these feelings, you shower the child with protection because in this way you prevent other people (and perhaps yourself) from knowing how you really feel. *Overprotection and overindulgence are not expressions of real love.* They are ways in which you conceal your real feelings. They take away the child's opportunity for learning how to take care of himself and for developing self-reliance and independence. As they grow up, children who have been overprotected and overindulged often become resentful of their parents. They realize that they have an additional handicap which might have been avoided.

THE WISHFUL ATTITUDE

Some of you, who find it hard to accept your child, develop an attitude of wishfulness regarding the problems presented by deafness. By your manner and attitude you seem not to want to admit to yourself that your child is deaf. So you act as though it is no handicap to be deaf. You show *no* consideration to your child because of his deafness. *No* allowances are made. You unrealistically ignore the difficulties which confront your child. Soon he begins to feel insecure and unhappy because he cannot live up to what you expect of him. He may become a show-off and very hard to train in his habits. He will try in many ways to please you because he *feels* how desperately you are trying to show that he has no handicap. Because you do not show him by your attitudes that it is not shameful to be deaf but that it does impose certain limitations which make adjustments necessary, *he too becomes wishful and unrealistic about himself.* Your attitudes must make him realize that the limitations imposed by deafness must be faced frankly. Unless he does, in later life he may not be able to face the restrictions which come from having impaired hearing. Such persons sometimes want to be musicians or want to enter some other field of work which is directly dependent on hearing. A deaf child has special needs because of his deafness. In this respect he is different and you should face this fact squarely as soon as possible.

ATTITUDE OF INDIFFERENCE

The fourth attitude which is common to some of you is the attitude of indifference. If you have this attitude toward your child you should seek assistance immediately in overcoming it. This attitude is especially damaging to your child. Your indifference means that you are not able to show your child real affection. You are lacking in sincere sympathy and genuine understanding of your child. Specialists sometimes refer to this attitude as the attitude of rejection; because of your feelings and points of view, without knowing it, you resent and reject your child emotionally. You may be critical of him and of anyone who attempts to point out your errors in handling him. Some parents can conceal these feelings so well that they are not recognized by anyone except a specialist in such problems. You may be genuinely concerned about your child's needs but because of your feelings you are not able to do more than to provide him with material needs. You cannot really enjoy him and give him genuine love and affection. At times this attitude of indifference is combined with frank hostility and open neglect of the child. Fortunately this is not common. Even those parents who openly neglect their deaf child usually find some reason for blaming the physician, a relative, the school, or community for their child's unhappiness.

Parents react to their child's deafness in a great many different ways. The four attitudes which have been considered simply illustrate some general ways in which parents have been known to react. It is clear that if you really understand your attitudes you will have a better relationship with your child. Your attitude is

important to him. Most parents know this and do their best to develop good wholesome attitudes.

It was stated above that it is not easy to develop good attitudes toward your child. Of course it can and must be done. There are several ways in which to proceed. It may help you to be more frank in discussing your feelings with your family and friends. Also, often it is wise to "talk it over" with your clergyman, family physician, a psychologist or a psychiatrist. These men can make many suggestions which will be helpful to you and to your child. Teachers and educators of the deaf also can give you information and advice which will help you with your attitudes and methods of handling your child. Many parents have been helped a great deal by discussing their feelings with deaf adults. If you make some inquiry you can get in touch with a deaf person who may give you some very helpful suggestions. Do not hesitate to contact anyone who is familiar with these problems. Many parents are now following such a plan. All parents of deaf children need some assistance. The longer you put it off, the more difficult it is for you to acquire the right attitude and to give your child the best possible foundation for his future happiness and success.

Chapter IV

THE DEAF CHILD AND HIS NEEDS

There are certain essentials of good training for all children. All children need affection, security, and consistent handling. They need to feel that they are wanted and that they are a part of the family. They need success, encouragement and wise discipline. They need to be reassured and relieved from fear after they have been frightened. They need freedom to play alone and with other children. They need to have their questions answered simply and frankly. They need praise, sympathy, and understanding. The deaf child is not different from the hearing child as far as his fundamental needs are concerned. The difference is that his needs must be met and satisfied in a different way. This means that his training must be more direct; concrete demonstrations are essential. He cannot be expected to pick up ways of acting and behaving through his daily contact with you to the same extent as does the child with normal hearing. He requires demonstration and careful explanation which takes much time and patience on your part. He can be trained very well if you will take the time, have the patience, and use methods which he can understand.

NEED FOR CONSISTENCY

One of your child's greatest needs is consistency. The child with normal hearing is constantly hearing explanations for things that happen. His world of happenings is tied together with language. In a typical busy household, father is late for dinner, mother gets a telephone call that he has been delayed by motor trouble, a report of icy streets is coming from the radio, the neighbors drop in to chat for a moment, a strange dog barks and runs down the driveway, and there is excited chatter because the neighbors down the street have a new baby. All of these happenings might be taking place at the same time.

These everyday happenings and experiences are united by the constant conversation and other sounds which are heard by the hearing child. To the deaf child these happenings are not united; they are not tied together by language. It is perhaps somewhat like what you would experience in a foreign country where you could not understand the language. However, even then you would have an advantage because you could learn much just from hearing sounds even though you could not understand the language. You must remember it is words that help us see how actions and attitudes are tied together. It is mainly through hearing that we see that there is meaningful consistency in the many happenings that otherwise seem to have no connection. Because the deaf child misses these hundreds and thousands of words and other sounds, his world needs direction in a consistent day by day manner. He learns what is expected of him, and that many happenings are related, by seeing them happen the same way again and again.

There are many ways in which you can be consistent and thereby help your child organize his experiences. You can arrange regular hours for his eating, sleeping, toileting, playing, and resting. Children like order and routine, especially deaf children. Regularity and routine will give your child a rhythm

35

of living which helps him to feel secure and that all is well. This is one of his greatest needs.

You can be consistent in showing affection. This too is a special need of your child because he more easily than the hearing child feels unwanted or that you are not pleased with him. It is hard for him to understand that we feel and act differently when a member of the family is ill. You must show him through words, gestures, and facial expressions why you are showing the feelings that you are; that your feelings are not related to anything he has done; the situation is one for which he is not to blame. You can make him understand that although you are not being directly affectionate to him it is not because you are not happy with him. However, he will become confused and bewildered if you are happy and jovial with him at times but at other times, for no apparent reason, you are short-tempered and impatient. He will develop feelings of being unwanted and he may either become overly active and aggressive or fearful and shy. Your child needs consistent affection from you and all members of his family.

You can be consistent in talking to him. Some parents have no trouble making themselves understood when they are alone with their child. When other members of the family or guests are present they find it hard to communicate with him. It is very common to see the child ask for explanations and want to be in on the happenings at such times, but the parents for many reasons do not bring him into the situation. Perhaps his mother is busy serving refreshments and his daddy is engaged in conversation about a recent fishing trip. Both parents ignore their child's curiosity and his desire to take part. This is one of the most common problems in handling the deaf child. You must be consistent and talk to him under all circumstances. This is discussed more completely in Chapter VI. We are concerned here only with the importance of consistency in talking to your child.

You can be consistent in your discipline. You should have rules and your child should be expected to follow them. If he is permitted to break the rules at times but required to follow them at other times he is always in a state of uncertainty. He cannot know when he is expected to follow the rules and when he is not. He always will be doing something (testing out the rule) to try to find out whether today is the day when he is expected to follow the rules. There is another aspect of being consistent in your expecting him to follow the rules. You must be consistent in your treatment of him when he has broken the rules. Your child must know what to expect when he has done something which requires discipline. He should not be disciplined for pushing books off the desk on Monday and then permitted to do so on Tuesday.

A mother asked what to do about her deaf child who persistently climbed on top of the refrigerator. In talking to this mother it was learned that the child had been permitted to climb on the refrigerator at certain times but not during the preparation of meals. Of course, the child did not know when she would be permitted to play in this manner and when she would not. She soon realized too that at times when she climbed up on the refrigerator, the family came running after her. Later, of course, she knew this was a way of getting attention.

You should not have many rules. The ones you have should be used consistently. Your child should be corrected only when he is expected to obey. Saying "no" in such a way that he does not know that you expect him to obey is teaching him to have no regard for your authority. You must expect your child to learn to be obedient in spite of his deafness. Being deaf should not excuse him from conforming to the usual regulations in your home. He can learn to conform if you consistently show him what you mean. If you wish him to conform you must have confidence in your demands, in yourself, and in your child. You should have a feeling of certainty and conviction about your requests. If you are uncertain when you correct him he will not feel that you expect him to obey. Believe in your demands and your child will follow them more readily. If you cannot come to a conclusion about what your rules and demands should be you should talk to someone who knows deaf children. Remember that consistency of handling will prevent many unpleasant situations. Consistency is the rule that you should follow in training your deaf child. He looks to you for direction; he likes to please you. He learns what to do and how to act to a great extent from the consistency you show in your handling of him.

NEED FOR BEING A PART OF THE FAMILY

Your child must be made to feel that he is a part of the family. He should feel that he is as much a part of the family as anyone else in it. You can give him this "sense of belonging" by building a bond between him and yourself. Help him to understand what is going on. Be happy with him, play with him, talk to him, and see that he takes part in your family routines. Try to understand his requests and give him real answers.

To realize how easy it is for your child to feel alone and misunderstood you must be aware of the importance of the thousands of sounds that are a part of our daily life. The deaf child who sees his parents in a playful scuffle does not hear the laughter and chatter that goes with it. He may think that you are quarreling. Imagine also that your family dog suddenly jumps on your child's lap. He begins to cry and to scream. You punish him for being "such a baby at his age." You do not realize that you heard the dog bark before he entered the room. You had been warned of the dog's coming but your child had not. When he is punished for these happenings, and most deaf children are at some time, he becomes fearful and confused. He may begin to question his place in the family. His hearing brothers and sisters do not get into these difficulties. This makes it seem as though he is not a part of the family in the same way as they are. Certainly this is one reason that many deaf children think that their parents show preference for their hearing brothers and sisters.

Although you should concentrate on keeping your child in close contact with the everyday happenings in your family you should not make him the center of attention. Because of his deafness you may feel that he should have everything he wants and that everyone in the family must cater to him. Many deaf children, through no fault of their own, find themselves playing the

part of little tyrants. They are permitted to take the toy, even though their sister is playing with it; they get the favors, such as candy and cookies; they are not expected to follow the same standards of discipline. Through such unnatural handling your deaf child learns to expect favors. He acquires a feeling that everyone is going to let him have his own way.

Naturally, the hearing brothers and sisters begin to resent him. Recently a mother stated that a hearing brother was frequently saying that he wished he were deaf. When the mother asked him why, he said, "Oh, you get everything you want and you don't have to mind." This is a most unfortunate attitude to have develop within the family. Both the deaf child and his hearing brothers and sisters are developing bad habits and attitudes. It is necessary to explain in a simple, matter-of-fact way to hearing children that because of his deafness the deaf child does require unusual attention in some ways. Your deaf child needs special consideration and handling in order that his needs be met. However, to make him the center of the family is as harmful and unwise as it is to neglect him. You must be aware that your urge to indulge him comes from your strong desire to overcome his being deaf. But the wholesome family for the deaf child is one where he knows he is wanted and understood; where he is shown consideration but where he assumes responsibilities and is not overindulged; where he is treated with respect and frankness but where he is expected to follow the same regulations as the other family members; where his good points and his bad points are accepted with sympathy and understanding.

NEED FOR SUCCESS

All children should be handled in such a way that they develop feelings of being successful. Through a sense of achievement and accomplishment they become self-confident and self-reliant. The hearing child who is handled well often does not need direct emphasis on being successful. This is not true of the deaf child, however. His deafness does make his adaptation to daily life more difficult. This increased difficulty of adapting begins very early in life. Perhaps it is being left out of the game in the backyard or just not being included in the "fun" as other children are. These are not great failures, but they happen day after day and when added together they become important to him. Soon he begins to compare himself with his playmates and to acquire feelings of not being successful. In other words, your child's deafness is a barrier to his being successful in a great many little ways. Even your own anxiousness about his *seeing* the cars as he crosses the street so he will not meet with an accident and your anxiousness about him in many other ways are experiences that convince him that he is different and not quite so capable as other children.

This is the natural limitation which is imposed by a serious hearing loss; it must be admitted and faced frankly. However, none of us will have only success. Furthermore no one can do all things with equal success. Everyone, through guidance from others and from his own experience, must learn to use his best abilities to be successful in a true sense. Your child, too, must learn not to dwell on his limitations but rather to emphasize his abilities. If he is afraid, lacking in confidence and unwilling to try new things, remember that he is not being stubborn; he is telling you that he needs more successful experiences so that he can overcome his fears of going ahead on his own. Do not insist on his doing things that depend a great deal on being able to hear normally. Direct his activities to action games, drawing, finger painting, and other types of play in which he can be as successful as any other child. Often children with handicaps which prevent them from doing certain things are even more successful than children without handicaps in activities which do not emphasize their disabilities. But you must be aware of the possibility that your child may develop real feelings of inferiority. You must be directly concerned about his developing feelings of being successful and competent. A very worthwhile way in which you can provide successful experiences for your child is through your habit training program. Habit training is discussed in Chapter V and will not be considered here. However, you should recognize that a child will feel as though he is failing if he is expected to dress himself before he is old enough to do so. Even more important for your child is the fact that he will feel inferior and unsuccessful if he is not taught to dress himself until long after his younger sister or his younger playmates have learned to do so. He makes an obvious comparison and knows that he is bigger but that he cannot do what they can.

The most satisfying experiences are those which are accomplished without reward or bribery. Your child will feel most successful when he shows you something which he has done on his own. You must express real interest in his accomplishments without giving too many suggestions or offering rewards too frequently. Suggestions rightly given often are helpful and desirable. Too much criticism and too little praise lead to feelings of not being able to do as well as one should. You must be genuine and sincere in providing ways for your child to be successful. Superficial success should be avoided. During your daily training and play activities there are a great many ways in which you can provide opportunities for developing feelings of success. You help him learn to use a spoon and later a knife and fork; you show him how to pull off his socks and how to put on his shoes; you show him how to roll and throw a ball; you show him how to use a pencil, how to make things from clay, and how to finger paint; you show him how to play with dolls and build with blocks. All of these activities and many others can be used as a basis for providing successful experiences. If you are aware of them and use them effectively, you are meeting one of your child's urgent needs.

NEED FOR ACTIVITY

All children are especially active before they learn to talk. Perhaps this is because they do not have words to use in the place of activity. In order to learn about an object which attracts them they must go to it, handle it, and perhaps taste it. After they have learned to talk they can use words in place of action and ask questions about it. Furthermore, they have very little experience to use in their solution of everyday problems and in overcoming the usual obstacles. As adults we have much less need for activity because we can use both words and past experience in overcoming our daily problems. The young child cannot sit down and think through the problem; rather his thinking is in the form of movement. He tries a great many movements until he satisfies his curiosity for the moment. Suppose that a child has awakened from a nap. He wants to open the bedroom door but finds that he cannot do so. He does not stop to think how the problem can be solved. He runs around the room, often pushing things down as he runs, and finally he may lie on the floor and kick and cry. Another example is that of the child who goes from one object to another, picking them up, holding them momentarily, perhaps putting them into his mouth, and then throwing them down and going on to more objects. This is the child's way of gaining experience and learning about his surroundings. He is using movement to a great extent as a substitute for words.

A great many parents ask why their deaf child is so active. Perhaps you have asked this question about your child. Some parents have found this to be one of their most difficult problems. From the above, you can see that the normal child is especially active until between two or three years of age when he has learned to talk and has less need for activity. The deaf child does not learn to talk at this age so his activity does not lessen. Often he becomes more active because he is more curious and has greater need for activity in order to satisfy his curiosity. You must recognize this important characteristic of your child as compared to the child with normal hearing. You should expect him to be more active. *This is normal for him.* He is using activity as a means of thinking, as a means of learning, as a means of keeping in contact with what is happening about him. He is using activity as a substitute for speech. As he learns to speak and to read your lips this need for movement and activity becomes less and less.

In some instances deaf children are unusually active not only because they lack speech but because of a combination of other reasons. It may be the result of inconsistent discipline, friction between the parents, the feeling of not being wanted, not understanding what is required of them, being overindulged and

43

receiving too much attention, or a feeling of jealousy toward their brothers and sisters. It may be necessary for you to get assistance in finding the cause of the activity if it is extreme in your child. Usually, however, if you understand that deaf children have greater need for activity and proceed to direct your child accordingly, you will find that it is not a serious problem.

In the general handling of your child your emphasis should be on directing his activity rather than on keeping him quiet or on keeping him from being active. You should direct him so that his activity will help him to learn, to mature, and to derive satisfaction and happiness. You must use and develop *his* interests, not *yours*. He does not know the importance of being systematic and orderly in dressing himself or in putting away his toys. But if you make a game of these activities, include him as a partner, tell him to run with his toy and put it in the basket, you are directing his activity in a purposeful way. He will not only be interested but the whole experience will be much more meaningful than if you simply tell him to put away his toys.

The deaf child's activities should be about the same as those of the hearing child. However, in directing your child you should emphasize *action*. He likes to observe action as well as to take part in it. His activities must be suited to his age and to the special requirements of your household. Your emphasis should not be on caution and fear of his getting hurt because of his hearing loss. You should take advantage of his need to be active by providing him with as big a variety of experiences as possible. Afternoon walks, as soon as he is old enough, are very helpful. You can point out a great many things to him such as trees, cars, milk bottles, flowers, dogs and cats. You can help him to see the relationships between what he sees and the many happenings in the home. Taking him to see where his daddy works may be a very happy experience. As his experiences grow and he sees that the many happenings of the day are related his need for activity decreases.

The right kind of toys and a good place to play do much to help your child use his energy and find an outlet for his need to be active. Toys give him an excellent opportunity to try new things and to learn. Even simple games have much value for your child because through them he learns cooperation. For example, he can learn very early to wait for his turn in rolling a ball. Playing with your child and teaching him *how* to play games is not a waste of time. After he has been taught or at least given some direction, he should be expected to play with hearing children and to play the game as they do. Often through first training your child and through suggestion you can direct the children into games which are not entirely dependent on sound, but that are rather mainly games of action; tag and hide and seek are examples of such games.

As soon as your child can walk, he should have toys which require active play, such as pull toys, stuffed animals, dolls and rubber balls. Between the ages of two and four, a box of large blocks and a sand box are excellent. Outdoor play should be encouraged whenever possible. A small jungle gym, swings, and a slide will help a great deal.

NEED FOR INDEPENDENCE

Perhaps you have thought of your child as being more dependent on you than are his hearing brothers and sisters. In some respects this is true. It takes more time, more patience, and more direct effort to train and to bring up a deaf child. This kind of dependence on you is desirable.

There is another kind of dependence which is not desirable, however. Some parents do not give their deaf child enough responsibility. They think that because he cannot hear he should be spared regular responsibilities and hardships. Nothing is more harmful to his general welfare. *Therefore, an important part of the program of developing your child's independence is your own realization that he can be independent in spite of his*

45

deafness. Your reluctance to ask him to assume normal responsibilities and your practice of protecting him from everyday hardships becomes an additional handicap to him. You must understand that feelings of security and self-reliance on your part, and confidence in your child, give him the best possible background for becoming independent.

It is not necessary to protect your child from the ups and downs of everyday living. The parents of a deaf girl had a serious financial setback. Although Joan was 16 years of age her parents still were not in the habit of telling her about the everyday facts of their household. They did not tell her what this financial loss meant to the family. Joan knew that something was wrong. She became fearful and unhappy. She could not sleep at night and she did not want to associate with the other girls in the school she was attending. Through guidance of both the parents and Joan, by someone who understood the problem, it was possible to relieve this conflict. Joan was handicapped not only by her deafness but also by the way in which she had not been permitted to learn to meet difficulties. It would have been much better for her if her parents had not kept her so dependent on them. Joan complained rather bitterly that they still considered her a baby. Keeping your child informed and giving him responsibilities even during early life are requirements of his growing up and becoming independent. He should be taught to dress and to feed himself, to care for his toys, to stay out of the street, to go to the corner store, and to help around the house. This is the way that all children gradually learn to care for themselves and to become independent of their parents. If you do not allow your child to become independent he may develop a resentful attitude toward you and toward society in later life. Many deaf adults say that they could have accomplished more in life if they had been permitted to develop independence like their hearing brothers and sisters.

Your guiding principle in training your child to be independent is that he should be taught to do for himself everything that he *can* do for himself. This training can begin at one year of age and sometimes earlier. He should be helped when necessary, but whenever he is helped when it is not necessary he is being deprived of an opportunity to learn to do things for himself. Perhaps you, like many other parents of deaf children, will be surprised to see how much more he can accomplish and how much more independent he can be than you thought, when given opportunities.

HEALTH NEEDS

All children should have constant attention to their health. This attention should not be given in a manner that shows anxiousness and over-concern, but rather in a calm, common-sense way. Children should have good nutritious food and plenty of fresh air, exercise, and sunshine. Regular sleep and rest periods are essential.

Most deaf children are not frail and in need of extra health care. Some children with impaired hearing do have special problems such as a discharge from their ears. If your child has a "running ear," you should take him to your physician regularly. You should follow the physician's advice rigidly. A discharge means that your child's hearing is gradually becoming poorer. Furthermore, the discharge might cause other health problems.

You should give your child's eyes especially good care. If the child with normal hearing loses some of his vision it is serious and a real handicap to him. If your deaf child loses some of his vision it is more serious because it means that he now has two disabilities instead of one. Your child's eyes also "hear" for him and are of utmost importance to him.

If your child became deaf from a serious illness or from an accident he may need more than average attention to his health. Otherwise, you should not be especially concerned about your child's health. But it is wise to take him to your doctor for a general examination about every six months until he is six years of age.

NEED FOR EXPRESSION

A child who cannot hear speech from the time of birth or who loses his hearing before he has learned speech will not learn to talk without special training. Perhaps one of your greatest concerns has been, "Will he learn to talk?" This question is discussed in detail in Chapter VI. However, we cannot conclude this chapter on the deaf child's needs without including his need for expression.

Speech is our main way of communicating with others. Most children at the age of three years can express themselves with great ease. If a child lacks the ability to speak easily and fluently it is disturbing to him. It is disturbing whether his speech difficulty is due to deafness or other causes. One reason that not being able to speak fluently is disturbing is that other people consider it peculiar. Many people who can speak normally look on those who cannot speak well as being odd, queer, and stupid. Your own reaction to your child's limited ability to speak is an important part of the problem he faces.

The child deaf from birth or early infancy is seriously handicapped in learning language. This is one of his outstanding characteristics. He cannot express himself and communicate in the same way as does the child with normal hearing. We have seen from the discussion of his need for activity that one way in which he attempts to express himself is through being more active. If you are alert to his need for expression you will see that he also finds other ways of expressing himself. He will use his voice in different ways to express different meanings even though he may not be using words. He will point to objects, to people, to himself, and he will use other gestures. Usually his gestures will be accompanied with meaningful facial expressions. At times when he is impatient or angry he may run, stamp his foot, or throw himself on the floor. You should remember that at times all children act this way. But because your child is deaf, these actions have a somewhat different meaning to him. He cannot speak to you in words so he speaks to you in other ways.

Communication means that one person has an idea which is expressed to another person; the two people understand each other because the first person has been able to make clear his thought to the second person. Our present day living emphasizes *speech* as the way in which to communicate to others; our culture and living habits are unusually dependent on the spoken word. This may cause you to over-emphasize the fact that your child cannot speak normally. You may forget that you can communicate with him without his being able to hear or to speak as you do.

Your child needs to express himself and to communicate with you in a real sense even in early infancy. You can convey meanings to him by your facial expressions, gestures, pantomime, and by actually dramatizing your ideas. You can "tell" him to "hurry" by walking fast or by running. Similarly you can "tell" him to "sit down," "go to sleep," and to do a great many other everyday activities. *It is of utmost importance to use speech constantly while you are "telling" him what you mean.* When you get him to understand what you mean he begins to realize that people do communicate and that it is possible for you and him to do so. It breaks down the barrier between you and your child. It develops his personality and makes him more social. Soon, of course, he will imitate you. This means that he is expressing himself and that he will be a much happier child. By giving him these beginnings of communication, you are laying the foundation for more formal and intensive training in speech and speech reading (lip reading).

Chapter V

LEARNING TO CARE FOR HIMSELF

We once asked the parents of a deaf child what progress they had made in toilet training their child. They hesitated for a moment; then the mother said, "We cannot train him; he does not understand us." Many parents have this mistaken idea that they can do little about training their child. It is more difficult to train a deaf child than it is to train a child who can hear. What you must remember is that you can make yourself understood; you can do a good job of training him. Most of you will find that you can do much better than you anticipated.

It is not surprising that some of you are fearful and concerned about how to train your child. Many of you have had only little experience with any children of your own and no experience with deaf children. Furthermore, perhaps you have been downcast and depressed about your child's deafness. Perhaps you think that a deaf child should not be expected to learn to care for himself, to learn to look after his own needs. If so, you must first realize that this is not true. *Your child can and must learn to care for himself.* You can train him to do many things for himself even in infancy and early childhood if you will but acquire the right attitude and if you will use methods which he can understand.

Before beginning the training program, you, his parents, must have overcome your feelings of sorrow and remorse about your child's deafness. Your child will not respond to your efforts if you approach him with a sad and depressed attitude. You must first enjoy him genuinely. You must approve of him and accept him as he is. This is essential to a successful training program. Worrying, forcing, urging, fussing and being impatient will make training difficult and bring unhappiness to you and your child. By enjoying your child, by being calm and matter-of-fact, by approaching him with sympathy and understanding, you will see results more quickly than you expected. Just a few demands at a time with well-timed directions and an abundance of praise should be your goal. Habits cannot be driven into your child. He can be trained by direction and encouragement. Happy parents can train well and happy children respond well.

Your entire attention and household routine should not center around your child. When this happens, he becomes demanding and self-centered. As he matures he should be taught to look after his own needs. From year to year he should assume his growing share of responsibilities. He should have certain duties and tasks to perform. The best home is one in which *all* members of the family share the responsibilities *and* the benefits of the household. Your child should not share in all the benefits without taking his share of the responsibilities and without making a real contribution to the family. He will do this best if he learns to do so little by little from early childhood.

All children vary in their readiness to learn certain habits. *Deaf children are no exception*. It is easy to forget that deaf children are different from one another just as are children who can hear. Every child has his own rate of maturing, of growing up. You must time your training to fit your particular child's rate of growing. You can do this by being alert to his interests, curiosities, and to his general growth and development. For instance, you must be aware that when he expresses an interest and a desire to feed himself by picking up the spoon and imitating you it is the right time to encourage him. This is the time to go along with him, to direct him instead of stopping him or continuing to feed him because you know that he will spill food on himself. Judging his readiness is very important because no amount of training will be successful unless your child is ready (sufficiently mature) to profit from it.

Although children vary in their readiness to learn there is an average age at which *most* children are successful in learning new habits. A child is not necessarily slow and mentally inferior just because he is a little below the average child in his development. Sometimes what happens to children causes their rate of development to vary from the average. Deafness is such a factor. There is some difference between the average age at which a deaf child learns certain habits and that of the child who can hear. The average deaf child is a little behind the average hearing child in learning to care for himself. This is not surprising. You should not be discouraged if this is true of your child. It is normal for the deaf child to mature a little more slowly. Because he does not hear he lacks some of the common experiences which help the hearing child to grow up, mainly the stimulation and challenge of language. You can do much to overcome this slight retardation. However, it will take time and effort because you must give him the experiences which are necessary to make him ready and mature enough for specific training. If you recognize this and do not get impatient and discouraged he will respond. In most instances all that is necessary is that you give him as many everyday experiences (play, contact with other children, freedom and encouragement to observe household and neighborhood activities) as you can and then give him a little more time to grow and mature. Your child is not below the average of the hearing child in his training because he is stupid or because you are inadequate parents and have not trained him well. You should expect him to learn to care for himself but you should expect it to take him a little longer to do so.

Because of his limitations in language it is sometimes hard to know when your child is ready for specific training. One way to find out if you should pursue certain training is to give it a trial in a straightforward, matter-of-fact way. You might say, "I am going to try to keep him dry this week. But if he does not understand, if he is not ready, I will let it go for a few weeks and then try again." Remember that success gives him confidence. If you keep trying and do not get results both you and your child will get discouraged. Also, when you do not get the results you expect you may try even harder to get him to respond. This irritates your child and causes you to develop a critical attitude toward yourself. You should be persistent but in a different way. You should make an attempt at training, but if your child does not respond, stop the training attempts. Give him experiences which help him to mature, watch for signs of readiness, and then try again.

All attempts at training should be simple and direct. You must be consistent; this means you should do the same from day to day at the same time. A simple but definite routine is necessary. You must be *concrete;* demonstrate the activities to him so that he can imitate you. The mother and father must agree on what to expect from their child. Disagreements, arguments, and different methods of handling are very confusing to him. Make every attempt at training a pleasant and successful experience for your child. Nagging, scolding, and shaming will not help him to learn and may even be harmful to later adjustment. Expect your child to make good steady progress but expect to give him more than average time and training.

In early infancy all children are entirely dependent on their parents. With normal abilities and opportunities they soon learn to do some things for themselves. As your child learns to care for himself he is also learning to be independent. With every step toward feeding or dressing himself he is taking steps toward developing an *inner* feeling of independence which is of utmost importance to him. This is sometimes called training for independence. *It is this inner independence which does so much for your child as he grows up.* This is training him in courage and self-confidence. When he learns to care for himself step by step, from pulling off his socks to buying his own clothing, gradually becoming more and more independent, he will not be overcome later by the difficulties in life. He is learning that he is capable of meeting and solving problems that arise in everyday living.

LEARNING TO EAT

Learning to eat is not a simple task for your child. Often you forget that the use of a spoon, a knife, or a fork requires good muscular coordination. Until your child has grown up enough physically he cannot use these utensils in the skilled act of eating. Children vary a great deal in their readiness to feed themselves. On the average they learn to feed themselves by the time they are three years of age.

Frequently parents do not train their deaf children to eat at the age at which they are ready for it. Many deaf children who enter nursery school at four years of age have had only slight training in feeding themselves. These children respond well to training. However, such training is often more difficult at four or five years than at the age of two to three. Your child is most interested in learning a new skill just at the time that he has matured enough to master it. After this, his interests shift to other activities. If you wait too long it is necessary to "bring him back" to learn something that he has missed.

Good eating habits cannot be forced on the child. You should not be anxiously concerned if your child does not immediately learn to feed himself. Neither should you be worried if your child feeds himself for a while, then again wants you to feed him. This is not uncommon. Usually it is only a phase in his cycle of growing up. Perhaps he is only trying out whether or not you would help him if he really needed it.

A mother asked us about her four-year-old deaf child's poor eating habits. In talking with her it was found that the time for dinner often varied by as much as an hour. Furthermore, there were happenings and confusions surrounding the dinner hour, especially when it was late, that caused Sally to not know what was expected of her. To even further complicate the experience for Sally, her parents on several occasions had sent her away from the table because of her misbehavior.

You should follow a definite routine for mealtime. Usually it is better to feed your child on schedule than to wait for members of the family who are late. If this is not practical at times, and if the wait is to be more than 15 minutes, a little snack often prevents restlessness which may result in poor eating habits. Regularity of eating is one of the essentials of good training.

Mealtime should not be a time of confusion, argument or play. It should be a happy time but hilarity is not conducive to good eating habits. Your child should not be threatened while eating; it is not wise to show him that if he does not eat his meat, it will be taken from him and given to someone else. All types of threats are undesirable.

To deny your child food at mealtime as a disciplinary measure is not wise. If he throws his cooky on the floor, you can show him that there are no more cookies until next mealtime. This is helping him to understand the natural consequences of his acts. This is usually sufficient for him to realize that he is not to continue with his unacceptable eating habits.

When your child is first learning to eat you should not be concerned about his spilling and making a mess. He must have practice in feeding himself. You should encourage him but you should not help him unduly. He should be praised for his attempts. You must realize that learning to eat is a slow process requiring great effort for the child. Sometimes he will tire and need help at the end of a meal. As he improves with practice your help should be discontinued.

The deaf child needs more demonstration of how to use a spoon, a knife, and a fork than does a hearing child, who learns a great deal from verbal explanations. You should use verbal explanations and say, "Now use your spoon like this." At the same time, you should be showing him how to handle his spoon. Nodding your head and using facial expressions of "that's good" will help him to try to imitate you. Usually it is more effective to demonstrate by using the spoon to feed yourself than it is to take your child's hand and try to show him in that way. You must not only be free of tension while you are training your child to eat, but you should have real feelings of enjoyment in your task and in your accomplishments.

Most deaf children present no special problem in learning to eat. They must be trained just as do all children. As the child reaches school age, there is a problem which often arises. Your child might eat very noisily because he does not hear the noise he makes in chewing his food. He does not realize that well-mannered people do not make a noise when they chew their food. He does not know that this is considered poor manners. He must be taught the fine art of eating noiselessly. This can be done. Usually all that is necessary is to point out to him that he should chew with his mouth closed.

Many parents are concerned about the eating habits of their deaf children. Some are concerned because they think their child does not eat enough. In talking with parents it has become clear that part of this concern is simply apprehension. Many of you have the feeling that because your child is deaf he must have other things wrong with him. Therefore it is easy to show too much concern about your child's eating habits. Soon your child realizes that you place an unusual emphasis on his behavior while he is eating. He learns that he can get favors and attention from you by the way he eats. This may continue until he has you performing a regular routine for him before he will eat. If your child presents an eating problem perhaps you should be more matter-of-fact and lay less stress on the way he acts while eating. Often it is wise to consult your doctor to check on what is needed in his diet.

TOILET TRAINING

It is somewhat more difficult to toilet train a deaf child than a hearing child. Deaf children as a group are slightly below the average in learning toilet habits. For example, more deaf children wet themselves at school age. The ease of communication between the parent and the hearing child is an obvious reason for this difference. Furthermore, often the hearing child hears you talk about toileting to his brothers and sisters. This helps him to be ready for training. The slight retardation of the deaf child in toilet habits should not be considered a weakness. It means that you should approach this training in a different way. If you show over-concern and apprehension about his training he will not readily respond to your training attempts.

You should not emphasize toilet training until your child is about a year and a half of age. When you begin your toilet training program you must keep in mind that your child must understand what is required of him. This can be accomplished by setting up a regular routine. Usually he will understand best when he is placed on the "toidy chair" in the same way at regular intervals. However, some children rebel at too much regularity. You must be careful not to place him on the chair too frequently. This should not be a play time. At first you should not expect him to remind you that he wishes to go to the toilet. Later, as he becomes familiar with the routine, he will take the responsibility of telling you. This occurs sometime during his second year.

Your child will not respond immediately to your attempts to train him. In some instances, after a few trials without any success, you may find it desirable to wait a few weeks before trying again. During the interval it may be helpful to note carefully the time of the day that he wets and soils himself. By adapting your program to his time needs it is often possible to make more clear to him what you are attempting to do. There are certain logical times to place him on the chair, such as after breakfast and after his naps. *However, the most important consideration from your child's point of view is that he learns what you mean by your attempts to train him.*

You should expect accidents to occur. After your child has been "dry" for several weeks or months he may again wet himself. Illness, new experiences, excitement, and many other factors play an important role in the control of his toilet habits. When accidents occur, he should not be punished or shamed; nor should he be made to feel that he is failing. The more successful he feels the better he will learn and the sooner he will be able to again control his toilet needs.

Often the toilet training program is rigid and inflexible. Parents frequently make a great deal of the toilet training. It is not uncommon for parents to make it such an important issue that the child rebels. He may feel that he is not living up to what is expected of him. A friendly, sympathetic attitude and a sense of humor do much to make training enjoyable for both you and your child.

DISCIPLINE AND PUNISHMENT

Part of growing up is to learn to respect the rights of others. Every child must learn that part of living effectively is recognizing that there are lines of authority. There is no complete freedom for anyone. We must learn that there are restrictions in homes and in society which are necessary for harmonious living. Perhaps the best kind of freedom comes from the knowledge that being mature and making worthwhile contributions in life requires an attitude of "giving" and of cooperativeness; an acceptance of all types of regulations which help people live, play, and work together. What a confusion and turmoil would exist if we did not have regulations and laws! We must all learn to control our own desires to a certain extent.

In early life children have no appreciation of the rights of others. Gradually, through training, they learn that their wants and desires must be modified to fit with the wants and desires of other people. You, like all mothers and fathers, are trying to train your child to respect the rights of others when you discipline him. You are trying to make him understand that there are certain ways of doing things which are considered good, and others which are not acceptable. All discipline should help the child understand his relationship to other people. It should help him to act more wisely the next time he is in the same or similar situations.

Unfortunately not all parents look at discipline in this way. *Often they do not realize that discipline should be positive, that it is a part of the total training that parents should give their children.* Some parents use discipline as a way of "getting even" with their child. They take the child's misbehavior as a personal insult which is directed at them. They discipline their child accordingly and say, "You put your candy on the tablecloth which mother just washed. Do you want mother to work so hard? Now you cannot have any more candy."

Some parents think of discipline only as a means of punishment. The child is punished for something which he has done, and no attempt is made to help him understand why. Discipline is used as a way of getting him to stop a particular activity without directing him into more suitable activities. He is punished in a way which causes him to become fearful and afraid of doing the same thing again. Often threats are used, such as "Now, if you do that again, I will send you away." This is getting the child to obey through fear. Threats often do cause children to obey, at least for the present. This method should not be used, however, because the fears remain with the child and may cause him to develop serious difficulties in later life. Good discipline always helps the child to see why his behavior is not acceptable; it helps him to learn to be responsible and to control himself.

Your deaf child requires discipline in the same way as do all other children. He too must learn that he cannot always have his own way and that there are restrictions and lines of authority which he must respect. He can learn to modify his demands and to fit into your home routines if you give him the necessary training in the right way. Many deaf children have not been well disciplined. Perhaps you do not require your deaf child to conform in the same way as you do your hearing children. The deaf child may have the "run of the house." He may not be expected to respect the "yes" and "no" lines of authority. He may be per-

mitted to become excessively demanding and self-centered; he may not be disciplined and directed in such a manner that he learns to have regard for the rights of others.

Your child will not realize what you mean when you first shake your head and say "no." It will be necessary for you to repeat and to point out that "no" is consistent with your own activities and with those of his brothers and sisters. What is *no* for him is also *no* for the other family members; what is *yes* for him is *yes* for the other family members. Some exceptions, of course, are necessary because of the different ages of the family members. In a few instances some exceptions occur because of the deafness itself. However, as a guiding principle, the yes and no limitations should be the same for all concerned. Your discipline must be consistent. If you are consistent in your demands and in your discipline in general your child gradually learns what is expected of him; he gradually conforms to the routine of your household.

Discipline should not be thought of as punishment. Rather, it should be considered as a means of helping your child to grow and to mature. Some restrictions and denials are a part of this approach. Your child must learn that if he does not conform to normal routines, he must expect certain consequences. *These consequences should be natural and not a means for the parents to exercise punishment.* For example, if your child walks into a mud puddle wearing his only pair of play shoes he should be expected to stay in the house and wait for them to dry. Also, if he is to have two pieces of candy a day and if he has both of them in the morning, he must be expected to wait until the next day for another piece. The natural consequences of an act are sufficient reprimand for your child, but you must see that he is aware of these consequences because his awareness of them is what makes them meaningful experiences. Slapping, threatening, shaking, and spanking should be avoided. These are outlets for the anger of parents. No discipline can be adequately given or handled in anger. Using discipline effectively is to help your child to learn to conform to the everyday restrictions of living. This can be accomplished only when it is done in a logical, calm, and sympathetic way.

JEALOUSY

To be jealous is to feel that others are going to take our place with those we love. In children it usually is a feeling that a brother or a sister is receiving more attention and affection than the child himself. Feelings of jealousy often do arise in deaf children. Most frequently it begins without your being aware of

63

it from the simple fact that your child's brothers and sisters (or playmates) can hear. They can respond to your calls from upstairs or out in the yard. They can make their wants and needs known simply and easily. Many deaf children, as they grow up, tell us that they want to hear. We know that often the child's real reason for wanting to hear is not so that he can hear the singing of birds, music, or many other sounds that you expect him to want to hear. He cannot have a desire to hear these sounds which he has not heard and knows nothing about. Many of these children want to hear because they are jealous of their brothers and sisters, or playmates, who can hear.

Ruth is an example. At an early age she showed indications of feeling inferior and jealous. She asked repeatedly for a hearing aid. Because she had no hearing a hearing aid could not be given to her; she could not be made to hear. She gradually became excessively persistent and demanding. Her teachers were finding her difficult to manage. In going over Ruth's problem with her parents we found that her hearing sister was winning many awards and honors in school. Naturally her parents were pleased and gave her much attention. Unfortunately, though, they compared Ruth to her sister. This made Ruth feel that she was not living up to her parents' expectations. She became jealous of her sister. She resented her. She said she wanted to hear so that she could do the same as her sister. She thought that in order to have the affection and attention of her parents she had to hear. Ruth's feelings were discussed with her parents. They refrained from comparing her with her sister and gave her much praise and affection. Gradually they were able to overcome her jealousy.

You can avoid the development of feelings of jealousy if you are aware that an obvious difference exists between your deaf child and his hearing brothers and sisters. You can overcome this difference by being consciously fair and considerate. It requires time, patience, and effort. At times your deaf child should be the first to be let in on a secret. He should not always learn about family "goings on" *after* his hearing brother and sister. Complete awareness of the situation with fairness and frankness will do much to prevent the development of feelings of jealousy.

A word of caution must be given regarding the development of feelings of jealousy in your children with normal hearing. Your deaf child in early life requires much of your time and attention. You must be careful not to allow this to cause his hearing brothers and sisters to feel left out.

FEARS

Hearing, perhaps more than any other sense, warns us of danger. For example, our ears tell us of sounds coming from all around us but our eyes can tell us only of what we can see in front of us. Because hearing is such an important warning sense your deaf child often is not warned about happenings as you are. Furthermore, he may not know or understand what is taking place around him. When he is confused and does not understand he may become fearful and apprehensive.

Fear is the feeling that all is not well; something bad is expected to happen. When we are fearful, we are also insecure. Feelings of fear and insecurity often can be dispelled by simply hearing sounds next door or down the street. Furthermore, sounds, especially speech, tie us together. When we hear familiar sounds and voices, although we may not be aware of it, we are less likely to be afraid. Speech also helps us to understand what things we should be afraid of and what things are harmless and need not be feared.

You may think that your child does not show enough fear of certain situations. Because deaf children do not hear they do not have some fears to the same extent as do hearing children. Some fears, such as fear of a hot stove, are desirable and necessary. Fears, both good and bad, are usually learned from hearing the parents speak about their own fears. Therefore, your deaf child may surprise you in showing no fear when you think he normally should be afraid. Likewise, he may be afraid when you can see no reason for his fear.

Your child will be frightened most easily by sudden movements, even the sudden appearance of a shadow. If he has some hearing he may be startled and frightened by a loud, sudden noise such as the slamming of a door. Also many children who are deaf have been hospitalized, which means that they have been separated from you. Separation is sometimes fraught with fear for the normal child; because it is more difficult to make the deaf child understand these experiences and the fact that mother and father will come back, he may become greatly frightened.

You must be aware of your child's fears. You should not insist that he go into a dark room if he is afraid. It is better to leave a night light burning in the hall near his room. Often it is helpful to leave the door to his room open. He will learn not to be afraid as he sees that you are not afraid and as he understands better. Many problems can be avoided by realizing that your child has fears. Accepting his fear in a matter-of-fact manner helps him to overcome it gradually. Shame, ridicule, comparisons with others, and punishment should be avoided. Whenever possible your child should be prevented from becoming unduly afraid.

TEMPER TANTRUMS, QUARRELING, AND STUBBORNNESS

The parents of a little deaf boy four years of age reported that he was difficult to manage. He had four or five temper tantrums a day. He was not eating and sleeping well. Naturally John's parents were concerned and wanted to determine the cause of his poor behavior.

There are many possible causes for temper outbursts. They may be caused by physical conditions such as earache, indigestion, and poor eyesight. It is wise to have a physical examination by your doctor, if your child has many tantrums. Tight clothing and poorly fitted shoes may cause tantrums. Excessive anger and tantrums can come from feelings of jealousy, loneliness, inferiority, confusion, insecurity, and many other psychological conditions. In deaf children tantrums occur most often because of the attitudes of their parents. Perhaps the parents are in conflict as to the best way of handling their child. This was true in the case of John's parents mentioned above. The mother had one way of handling John and the father handled him in an entirely different way. John became confused; he did not know what was expected of him. He was expressing his confusion and unhappiness by having tantrums.

Temper outbursts should be avoided whenever possible. Your child may have tantrums because he cannot make himself understood in any other way. Although this occurs in deaf children it should not be encouraged as a way of making his wants known. You should give him other ways for telling you what he wants and needs.

Quarreling between the deaf child and his brothers and sisters, or with his playmates, is rather frequent. When this is discussed with the parents they frequently describe the deaf child as stubborn. He is said to be aggressive, persistent, and determined. In going further into such situations it is usually possible to find the cause. In one instance it was learned that the children were calling David, the deaf child, "dummy." David's brother was a member of the neighborhood group but he of course could not withstand the influence of his group. David did not know what "dummy" meant but he sensed that he was not being accepted. He rebelled and became the child who was described as stubborn.

Temper tantrums, excessive quarreling and stubbornness are signs which tell you that all is not well with your child. Rather than punishing him for these acts you should find the cause of them. He does not want to be disagreeable. When you have found the cause and made changes accordingly, he will no longer need to have tantrums or be unduly quarrelsome. Tantrums, quarrelsomeness, and stubbornness should be prevented whenever possible.

NAILBITING AND THUMBSUCKING

Nailbiting and thumbsucking are among the most common problems mentioned by all parents. These habits are especially distressing to some parents of deaf children. As a group, deaf children probably bite their nails and suck their thumbs more than hearing children do.

It is not desirable to use force in trying to overcome these habits. Restraints, such as tying the child's hands or using mittens, are very disturbing and should be avoided. These habits suggest that your child is having difficulty in growing up emotionally. For example, perhaps your child is sucking his thumb or biting his nails because he feels that you are not happy with him as he is.

If these habits continue you should seek the help of a doctor in finding the cause. In general it is well to remember that a happy and emotionally satisfied child usually does not continue these habits. Also, all children in early life put things in their mouths. This is a normal growth process. You should be concerned only if it is excessive beyond the age of four or five years.

WALKING

Deaf children usually present no special problem in learning to walk. However, if your child became deaf in early infancy because of a disease which affected his balance (see Chapter II), he may be slow in beginning to walk. This may be true also if your child's deafness is due to a birth injury. Frequently these children are awkward and clumsy in their movements. Usually as their muscular coordination improves, this becomes less noticeable.

Deaf children do have a characteristic way of walking which many parents find annoying. The deaf child's manner of walking can be described as a "shuffling gait." As he walks he scrapes his feet, especially his heels, on the floor. Perhaps you have asked your doctor, "What causes him to drag his feet?" The reason that deaf children walk in this manner is not clearly understood. One reason might be that they do not hear the "shuffle." Perhaps hearing children lift their feet more and prevent shuffling because they hear the noise it makes if they do not. Again, conscious effort on your part will help your deaf child to learn to walk by "picking up his feet." In a frank and sympathetic way, you should show him how you walk. Marching games in which you lift your feet high will help him to emphasize that "shuffling" is not the way to walk. Your child will like such games. He will also gradually learn to walk without shuffling his feet.

NOISY BREATHING AND VOCALIZING

A common characteristic of deaf children is the noise they make when they breathe. This "noisy breathing" sometimes continues into adulthood. Like the shuffling gait of the deaf child, noisy breathing is perhaps a direct result of inability to hear. When hearing is normal the child senses in early life that people normally breathe without much sound. Your child, of course, does not know that he is making more sound than you do in breathing. He can be trained to breathe with less noise but usually this should not be attempted until the age of five or six, or even later. You should not make him self-conscious about his breathing. If relatives or friends inquire about it, a simple explanation of why it occurs is usually all that is necessary.

Perhaps your child makes sounds with his voice without being aware of the kind of sound it is or how loud it is. This vocalizing is sometimes annoying. We learn to control our voices through hearing others use their voices. Often a deaf child, like many hearing children, learns that he can get attention by screaming or otherwise using his voice. Again, your attitude and the way you correct him is extremely important. He needs to vocalize and he will learn to control his voice. If you reprimand him and cause him to become fearful of using his voice it will be more difficult to teach him to speak.

SLEEP AND REST

All children require adequate rest and sleep if they are to be healthy and happy. Children vary a great deal in their need for sleep and rest. You can and should determine the amount of sleep needed by your child. Expecting him to sleep more than he needs is to invite difficulties.

The parents of Dick, a three-year-old deaf boy, asked advice regarding his going to bed. Dick would not stay in bed. Often his parents would spend one to two hours coaxing and trying to persuade him before he would finally stay in bed and go to sleep. This is a rather common complaint of parents of deaf children. A problem such as that presented by Dick does not arise suddenly. It develops over a long period of time. If your child's sleeplessness is not caused by physical conditions, it results from poor handling and poor habit training. For example, Dick's parents did not have a regular hour for him to get ready for bed. Furthermore, Dick had been successful in using many ways to persuade his parents that he should not go to bed or that he should get up again after he had been put to bed. The parents without realizing it were encouraging his activities.

In establishing habits of sleep and rest, routine is particularly important to your deaf child. A regular hour for naps and for going to bed at night will help him to know what to expect. Getting ready for bed should be a happy time but not a time for boisterous activities. Playing with blocks and looking at picture books (the pictures should not be frightening) are activities well suited to the hour just before going to sleep. Consistency in your routine will do much to help your child acquire a good attitude toward sleep and rest.

NEIGHBORS AND PLAYMATES

One of the most common complaints of parents of deaf children is that the neighbors do not accept their child. This is particularly true if your child has difficulty in getting along with the children in the neighborhood. Unfortunately, some people will not understand and will have little sympathy for your child. Usually, however, if your child is not excessively demanding and if you have trained him to give and take in a real life way, you can overcome the attitude of strangeness on the part of the neighbors. Certainly there are exceptions. Many crowded apartment conditions make the handling and training of a deaf child extremely difficult. In such circumstances the most desirable solution is to find more suitable living quarters if at all possible.

You should discuss your child's deafness frankly with your neighbors. Explain your training program to them. Frankness and sincerity will help them to understand. If they see that you can manage your child and be happy with him they will accept him much more readily. On the other hand, if you are defensive and never admit faults in your child they will not accept your child easily. You should not expect your child always to be the center of attention; he should not win at all of the games because he is deaf. He should learn to take his share of "knocks" in the play yard without interference from you. Neither should he always be the loser. He must not be the object of ridicule.

Neighborhood difficulties should be completely eliminated. You cannot do the best for your child if you are fearful about the attitudes of your neighbors. An honest, straightforward, sympathetic approach on your part usually eliminates the fear and misunderstanding your neighbors display.

Chapter VI

LEARNING TO COMMUNICATE

W ill he learn to talk?" This is the parents' most common question when they learn that their child is deaf. You may have asked this question too. Perhaps a definite "yes" should be given in answer to your question at the very beginning of this discussion. He will learn to talk. But there is much variation in the naturalness and in the perfection of the speech of deaf children. Some learn to speak much better than others. Some never learn to speak well enough so that they can talk with ease to those unfamiliar with their speech.

There are many reasons for this difference among children in learning to speak. We shall consider some of these reasons in this chapter; then you can better understand your child's difficulty in learning to communicate. Speech reading, the ability to understand what the speaker says by watching him, will be discussed separately from speech. Nevertheless, you must remember that your child is fulfilling only one half of the art of communication when he makes himself understood through speech. Unless he has sufficient residual hearing to be able to hear speech he will be dependent on speech reading in order to complete the act of communicating. Communication is always a two way process. He must be both a speaker and a "listener." Your child will use his eyes for "listening" and for understanding what is said to him.

YOUR CONCERN ABOUT SPEECH

Ease of communication is the greatest difference between your child and the child with normal hearing. The normally hearing child between two and three years of age has a flow of speech which is marvelous when compared with the child who has been deaf from infancy. Perhaps you have been distressed by this comparison. Certainly all parents are concerned about their deaf child's learning to talk. You may be more concerned about his speech than you are about his deafness. Apparently not being able to speak is more noticeable than not being able to hear. Also, your child's lack of speech is more distressing to you than is his not being able to hear.

Your concern about your child's speech is desirable; you should be concerned about his greatest difficulty, that of learning to communicate. However, in his learning to communicate, just as in all of his training, overconcern will retard instead of help your child. We now know that much more can be done to develop speech during the early years of life than was thought to be possible some years ago. This does not mean that going to an extreme and forcing speech development is good for your child. Because of his deafness he is in a sense isolated from you and the daily happenings in your home. By your concern about his speech you are trying to bridge this gap between your child and yourself. But by overconcern, by overemphasis on speech, it is possible to cause the barrier between you and your child to become greater rather than to become less and less. You can help him with his speech. However, speech development will parallel his physical, social, and emotional maturity. If you have trained him well in other respects, if he feels secure and confident, emphasis on speech will be more successful and more meaningful to him. If he has been poorly trained and disciplined, if he is insecure and fearful, your emphasis on speech will cause him to be more unmanageable.

Emphasis on speech and speech reading can and should be started early. Too early emphasis on formal training may be to your child's disadvantage. You should first give him a broad foundation of experiences. Help him to learn that communication is possible. Allow him to express himself through gestures if he wishes. Also, try to understand his vocalizations without expecting or demanding speech in the usual sense. Remember that the normal child uses gestures, such as reaching and pushing, together with vocalizations to express himself long before he uses speech. When you see your child communicating in this way give him encouragement and "talk his language" with him. *Of course, you should be using speech while you are encouraging and helping him to express himself*. The difference is that you are not demanding that he use speech as you use it. This is not possible for him at first.

Speech is based on concepts and meanings. Words are used as symbols to express a mental picture. The word "ball" means a particular round object with which the child has played; personal contact and experience has been had with the object. Until your child has had many experiences with objects and people and therefore has a need for words any attempt to train him to use speech is meaningless.

THEIR ABILITIES VARY

It is hard for you to think of deaf children as being different one from another. The common problem of deafness obscures the differences between them. Therefore, when you see a child who has learned to speak well you may think that all deaf children talk as he does. If you see a child who has developed very little speech you may think that no deaf children can learn to talk. In reality, each child must be considered as an individual. There are perhaps even wider differences between deaf children than there are between hearing children. Deaf children, in addition to being different in such ways as their capacity to learn, have differences in the degree of hearing impairment and the age of becoming deaf.

One reason for the wide differences in deaf children's speech is that they vary in their abilities and temperaments. Some deaf children learn speech more readily than others because it is easier for them to do so. It seems to be similar to learning to play the piano. Some children, because of their aptitudes and abilities, find it easy; they learn to play the piano very well. This is a small group of children. A large group of children learn to play in an average way because they have average ability. Then there is another small group which, in spite of effort and training, cannot play the piano so well as the average child or the talented child. They do not have the required ability to the same degree. Experience tells us that deaf children respond to speech training in somewhat the same manner. With few exceptions they all learn to talk but some much better than others.

SOME HAVE RESIDUAL HEARING

Another reason for differences in speech is that some children have hearing which can be used. If your child has some hearing he may be said to have residual hearing. Residual hearing refers to the hearing which remains; that hearing which is present although the hearing is not normal or average. When there is sufficient residual hearing so that sounds can be heard when they are made louder, it is tremendously helpful in speech training and development. Because of improved methods of testing hearing and because of the great improvement in hearing aids it is now possible to make use of even small degrees of residual hearing. This is one of the major developments in recent years in the education and training of children with impaired hearing. How to make use of residual hearing is discussed under auditory training.

TESTS OF HEARING

Perhaps you have asked your doctor about your child's residual hearing. If not, you will at some time want to know how much hearing he has. In finding out how much hearing remains the

doctor determines your child's hearing acuity. He finds the faintest sound that your child can hear. This can be done completely only after he is about five years of age. However, some measure of his hearing can be made at one year of age and sometimes even earlier. The doctor, who is trained and experienced in using different types of loud sounds, called free-field tests, can make a good estimate of the residual hearing. On the basis of such tests he can make suggestions on how to proceed in working with your child. Also, research on tests of hearing for very young children is continuing and perhaps in a few years it will be possible to determine exactly the amount of hearing present at a very early age.

After about five years of age it is possible to do a complete hearing test with an audiometer. This is an instrument used to produce sounds of various pitches or frequencies. In Chapter I frequency was described as the number of times that a sound vibrates in one second. With the audiometer it is possible to test your child's hearing for several frequencies which are known to be most important in hearing speech and other everyday sounds. These various frequencies of sound are called pure tones. By using pure tones it is possible to find more exactly what sounds your child hears and what sounds he does not hear. For example, noise consists of a mixture of many frequencies, both low and high pitch sounds. If we use such sounds to test your child's hearing we cannot determine whether his hearing is better on high or low pitch sounds. With the audiometer test only one frequency is used at a time, not a mixture of frequencies. This is why it is commonly called a pure tone test.

Another advantage of the audiometer test is that it is possible to make the sounds as loud as is practical. When the sound is made as loud as possible on the audiometer it is to the limit of practical or usable hearing. This means that if the sounds are made as loud as they can be on the audiometer and your child does not hear them he has no practical or usable residual hearing. In this case he is rightly referred to as a deaf child. While he might have small remnants of hearing this hearing cannot be put to practical use. Even though powerful hearing aids are tried he does not gain enough from them to make it worthwhile to use them.

The audiometric test usually consists of finding the faintest sound that your child can hear for seven different frequencies from 125 to 8000 vibrations per second. Finding the faintest sound he can hear is called determining his threshold. The point at which he can just hear each frequency is marked on a card made for this purpose. These points are connected by a line and this graph of his hearing is called an audiogram.

If your child has some understanding of speech through hearing, carefully constructed speech tests can be used to test his hearing. These tests show how well your child hears and understands speech as compared to how well he can hear pure tones. These tests are especially helpful in evaluating the possibilities and advantages of his using a hearing aid. Some understanding of speech must be developed before such tests can be used.

It is possible to test the hearing of children in groups. These tests are very useful for large public schools. They are called screening tests. Their purpose is to find children who have hearing losses that have not been recognized. When these children are found early and medical treatment is given, further hearing loss may be prevented and often lost hearing is regained. These programs for identifying children with mild hearing impairments and preventing hearing losses in others are called hearing conservation programs. Fortunately more and more local, county, and state hearing conservation programs are being established every year.

THE USE OF HEARING AIDS

If your child has enough hearing to profit from the use of a hearing aid it will be much easier for him to learn to speak. Being able to hear sounds, even if only loud sounds, is very helpful in the development of speech. Whenever possible a hearing aid should be used because it is the best method known for helping your child to learn to talk. There are children who do not have enough hearing to use a hearing aid. How they are taught speech will be discussed later.

There are two types of hearing aids. One is the wearable type. This is to be worn by the individual. Perhaps you have seen these hearing aids because they are now commonly used by children and adults. The other type of hearing aid formerly was called a "desk" model. More recently it has been called a home training unit or an auditory training unit. This instrument is not to be worn; it is placed on a table. It has earphones to be put on your child only while you work directly with him. This type of hearing aid has been especially made for practice in listening and in learning to use residual hearing.

Only rarely is it possible to use a hearing aid of any kind before the child is two years of age. Between one and two years of age you can talk to him close to his ear if he has a considerable amount of hearing. By carefully trying over a period of time you can find how close to his ear you should be and how loud you must talk. You should not shout in your child's ear. *Constant talking close to his ear may be of great benefit to him.*

Experience has shown that the use of a wearable hearing aid is largely limited to after four years of age. Furthermore, it is much easier for your child to use a portable hearing aid if he has first had training on a home unit. This means that you can help your child with speech development by using a home training unit, particularly when he is between two and four years of age. This must be done with care and in a way that will not cause your child to develop the wrong attitude toward such training. If he has enough hearing to use a hearing aid when he enters school, and also in later life, it is extremely important that he have a good attitude toward it. Your attitude toward his use of the hearing aid will be important in developing your child's attitude.

Some parents overemphasize the use of the auditory training unit. When they do not get immediate results they double their efforts and try to force the child to go through long practice periods. Also, these parents become apprehensive and anxious about the child's progress. Such an approach might be very damaging to the child. Children between two and four years of age should not be expected to take part in rigid and formal "lessons" in hearing. Rather, the approach must be informal and game-like. The periods must be very short, preferably five minutes, and should concentrate on one sound for each period.

Whenever possible you should have someone who is familiar with the use of hearing aids and auditory training methods to help you in getting started. It is not necessary for you to be a specialist in order to be of help to your child. It is, in fact, more important to be real fathers and real mothers. The importance of patience, love, and understanding cannot be overemphasized, as a part of teaching your child to use the hearing aid. Hearing aids are of great importance when they can be used, but they should not be expected to solve all problems. They should be considered a very important part of a broad, systematic approach to the development of speech and to overcoming the problems caused by a hearing loss.

SPEECH READING

Speech reading is often called lip reading. Speech reading is a better name for this ability because it more correctly describes what is done. Speech reading means the ability to understand what the speaker says by watching him. Special attention is given to the speaker's face and lip movements but facial expressions, gestures, where the conversation is taking place and many other "cues" are important to the speech reader.

Speech reading is a rather difficult skill to master. Nevertheless, it is surprising to see how many children with impaired hearing learn to do some speech reading even without special training. Children vary in their ability to speech read just as they vary in their ability to master any other skill. All children with hearing losses learn to do some speech reading. Some learn this skill so well that they seldom misunderstand what the speaker says. Some understand so well in this way that the hearing speaker is not aware that his "listener" may be understanding him entirely by watching him and not by hearing him.

It is possible for your child to begin understanding you through speech reading at about two years of age. He begins by gradually becoming aware that your lip and facial movements have meaning. It is of course necessary that you have him look at you when you are talking. This is difficult for your young child and you must not expect him always to look at you when you want him to do so. He will gradually learn to watch you when you are speaking. You should take advantage of times when he looks at you to use a simple sentence such as "Come on," "Give it to me," etc. Through constant repetition he gradually learns that your lip movements have meaning.

You should talk to your child constantly just as though he can hear you normally. At times you may take a specific object, such as his ball, and while casually playing with him call his attention to your face as you say "throw the ball," "big ball," etc. Use objects which your child knows and with which he has had experience.

Another way to stimulate his speech reading is to use the words for specific actions, such as run, jump, peek, and fall. Demonstrate clearly each activity and then immediately call attention to your face as you say the word. Gradually he will learn to imitate you and to perform the various acts, as he sees you say the words for them. Considerably later, perhaps between three and four years of age, you can expect him to respond to names of brothers and sisters and to his own name. Contrary to what you might have thought, learning to speech read names, including his own, is more difficult than simple exercises such as given above. As he progresses you can gradually increase the difficulty of the words and sentences, going from the concrete to the more abstract; gradually you should go from sentences such as "This is an orange" (concrete) to "I like oranges" (more abstract).

Remember that it is impossible for your child to speech read unless he can see you. Good light is essential. The light should be on your face and not shining directly into his eyes. Speech reading from the side is much more difficult than from the front. Obviously speech reading cannot be done from the back. Furthermore, it is very hard to speech read a speaker who is not at close range. For the young child three to four feet seems to be the best distance.

You cannot force your child to learn to speech read. With direction and encouragement you can help him acquire the fundamentals. He will continue to improve in speech reading. You can lay the foundation for the further training he will get when he enters school. Again, it is not the specialized training you give him that is most important. Rather it is the confidence, courage, and stimulation which you give him that makes it possible for him to progress more easily in school. If you over-emphasize your role as teachers and do not fulfill your role as parents your child will have more difficulties than if you did not try to do any special training. Your greatest task, challenge and opportunity is to be your child's parents. This is more difficult than being his teacher.

THE CHILD WHO HAS NO HEARING

When Larry was between two and three years of age his parents brought him to the hearing clinic to find out whether he had any residual hearing. He was well trained and able to cooperate very well. Many noise tests were used. Very loud sounds were made close to his ear. Larry did not respond to any sounds. His parents were told that talking close to his ear or using a hearing aid would not help him. Larry was deaf in the true sense of the word. There are many children like Larry. You may have been informed that your child has no residual hearing.

The amount of residual hearing should be ascertained as soon as possible. If your child does not have enough hearing to profit from a hearing aid he should not be expected to use one. Expecting him to do the impossible is simply making him fail. Some of you may persist in getting and using a hearing aid even after you have been told that it cannot help your child. This is unfortunate for him. It would be better for you to say "If he has no hearing, I will handle him accordingly; I will not expect him to do what is impossible."

If your child cannot hear, you can help him to begin speech reading. Furthermore, it is important that you encourage him to use his voice. Like other children with hearing losses, he will learn to call you and to use his voice in other ways. Vocalizing should be encouraged. From three to four years of age you can give him simple words by speech reading in a game-like manner and encourage him to imitate you. All of his attempts to repeat the word should be praised.

You can show him that he can *feel* sound. Take his hand and place it on your nose as you make the sound "m-m-m-m-m." Then place his hand on your throat as you make the sound "bu-bu-bu-bu." After doing this for short periods of time place his hand on his nose and on his throat and indicate that he should imitate you. Make these exercises enjoyable games. Do not be concerned about the results at first. Gradually he will imitate you; gradually you can use other sounds and simple words. Most importantly you will make him aware that he can use his voice in a meaningful way. Later he will learn to control it and to use it more effectively.

Perhaps you should be cautioned that these exercises in themselves will not give your child speech. They are simply the beginnings. Rightly done they will be helpful to him when he enters school for more intensive speech training.

It is more difficult to teach a child to speak when he has no hearing. The child without hearing can learn to speech read as well as the child with residual hearing. However, from research studies and from experience we know that usually the child who is deaf from infancy has the most difficult time with all other aspects of communication; he has the most difficulty in learning to speak, to read and to write. If your child has no hearing you should accept this greater difficulty realistically; your plans and expectations for him must be made accordingly. You will find that he will be as capable in other ways as the children who have some hearing.

AUDITORY TRAINING

Auditory training means training in the use of the hearing which remains, so that sounds which are heard can be understood. One way to think of the need for auditory training is to imagine what would happen if a person who had never heard suddenly became able to hear normally. All of the hundreds of sounds that are so easily recognized and understood by everyone who has normal hearing would be simply a confusion of noises to the person who had never heard them before. He would have to learn that the "honk" came from an automobile, the "cackle" from a hen, and the "moo" from the cow, and the "chatter of voices" from people. He would have to learn that our stream of vocalization has meaning, that we call these sounds speech. It would not take much time for this person to learn the difference between the roar of the airplane motor and the crow of the rooster. The difference between these two sounds is great and recognizing this difference is called the ability to make **gross auditory discriminations.** It would take much more time to learn the difference between "He ran to get the sheep" and "He sang her to sleep." Recognizing the difference between these two sentences is called the ability to make **fine auditory discriminations.**

The baby with normal hearing soon learns to make gross discriminations. At a few months of age he knows the difference between the voice of his mother and the sound of the dog barking. At about one year he discriminates the sounds of one word at a time; he knows such words as "no," "baby," and "candy." At about two years he has learned to discriminate between the sounds in short sentences. For example, now he knows the difference between "Get the ball" and "Show me your shoe."

. Your child, when he first hears through a hearing aid, or when you first talk close to his ear, will not know what the sounds mean. He, like the person who suddenly acquired normal hearing, will have to learn to discriminate between sounds, to learn how they are different and also to learn their meanings. Like the baby with normal hearing, he will first learn the difference between sounds that are very different; later he will learn the difference between words such as "run," "no," "jump," and "ball"; finally he will learn to discriminate between words in sentences.

Auditory training usually should be accompanied by training in speech reading. Allowing your child to see your lip movements and your facial expressions helps him to get meanings. In this way you are getting his eyes and ears to work together. *When you use both "seeing" and "listening" at the same time he will get a stronger impression than if you use his eyes and ears separately.*

Gradually your child will learn to tell the difference between sounds and to associate the meaning with the sound. As he progresses he may even correct you, as Jo Anne corrected her teacher one day. The teacher had been doing auditory training and using "quack, quack" for the sound made by ducks. One day Jo Anne through her hearing aid heard real live ducks. She noticed that the sounds they made did not sound like the "quack, quack" made by her teacher. She told her teacher about it; she wanted to know why. This gave the teacher an opportunity to explain that sounds like "quack, quack," "meow" and "bow-wow" were not the real sounds but simply imitations to stand for the real sounds. In this sense they are like any other words, simply substitutes or symbols for that which they represent.

In auditory training, just as in all other training of your child, *it is essential to use his interests and experiences as your foundation and starting point.* He is not an adult; adult ideas and experiences are foreign to him. Furthermore, his experiences are different because he does not hear normally. You must know your child and begin with him, not with your own experiences or interests.

To a great extent the amount of hearing which remains determines the success of the auditory training program. If your child's hearing loss is moderate he will not only develop better ability to understand and to use speech, but he will do so in less time than the child with a severe loss of hearing. All children who can use hearing aids must have auditory training to get the best results from them. You can use a great many natural sounds to get your child interested and to develop his ability to discriminate. The sounds made by doors, playing with pots and pans, bells, drums, clapping of hands, and many others, can be used. Some auditory training units have phonograph attachments which make it possible to use the many records now available for young children. If these are skillfully selected, by recognizing the difference between gross and fine auditory discriminations, they are most helpful. It must be emphasized, however, that most records for children with normal hearing are based on an understanding of language and as a result are very difficult for the child who is just learning to hear.

THE CHILD WHO LOSES HIS HEARING

Many children lose their hearing through illness. In Chapter II we discussed the importance of the age at which deafness occurs. If your child loses his hearing after he has learned to talk usually he will retain his speech if he is given encouragement and assistance. It is not easy to train a child to continue to use his speech after he loses his hearing. Again, if he can use a hearing aid, it is quite different because he can be made to hear speech. *If he has no residual hearing he must learn to control his voice by learning how it feels when he talks.* His speech will not be like it was before he lost his hearing. This is to be expected because hearing is the only sense which gives us direct control of our speech. If your child loses his hearing before two years of age the problem of speech training is very much the same as that of the child deaf from birth. If he loses his hearing after two years of age but before five years of age the speech will be retained within certain limits and it will be an advantage to him. If he loses his hearing after five years it is not so difficult to retain good speech. The longer he has heard before losing his hearing the easier it is for him to keep his natural speech.

The child does not lose his speech because his voice has been affected by the illness or injury that destroyed his hearing. His speech changes because he can no longer hear himself and others speak. This is why it is so important to keep the child talking immediately after he has lost his hearing. If he is not kept talking and if he does not continue to have a need for his speech, it will be much more difficult to develop speech again after he has forgotten it.

The child who loses his hearing needs assistance in other ways. This was discussed in Chapter IV.

OVERCOMING THE PROBLEM OF COMMUNICATION

The difficulty of communication is the greatest problem which faces your child. If his hearing loss is severe you should expect him to have some difficulty in communicating. Having and using a hearing aid is not the same as having normal hearing; being able to speech read is not the same as being able to hear speech; learning to speak without normal hearing is a slow, difficult process and will not result in perfectly normal speech. Some children with severe hearing losses overcome the communication hardships unbelievably well. Usually there is a communication difficulty which persists irrespective of what is done. This does not mean that you and the educators have failed. A great deal has been accomplished. *It is possible, however, for you and the educators to expect too much.* Deafness in infancy is a handicap which especially affects the ability to communicate. It is not possible to overcome it completely and to give your child the easy natural way of communicating which is characteristic of hearing children. This means that it is necessary for your child to learn to live with certain limitations which are imposed by his deafness. There are a great many ways in which you can help your child in learning to live happily and successfully even though he may not be able to communicate normally, as compared to his hearing brothers and sisters.

GOING TO SCHOOL

As you work with your child you look forward to the time when he will be old enough to enter school. You know that this is the time when you and your child will have the expert assistance of a trained teacher of the deaf. Many schools now have a nursery department and accept children at a very early age. If your child is emotionally secure and well trained, the

earlier he can associate with other children and the better it is for him. If you cannot enter your child in a special school until he is four years of age or older, you may be able to enter him in a regular nursery school for hearing children in your community. This has been done very successfully by some parents. Usually this is done between the ages of three and four, or three and five years. Being in a group and learning to play with other children is helpful to him. Both you and his teacher must be alert to his needs and give him direction in getting along with hearing children. As soon as he is old enough it is desirable to enter him in a special school where the teachers are trained to teach deaf children.

There are two types of schools for deaf children. One is called a **Day School.** This is a school which operates on the same schedule as schools for hearing children. The child lives at home. He goes to school during the usual hours and then returns home, just as the hearing child does. The other type of school is called a **Residential School.** As the name implies, in this school the child lives at the school. Children may go home weekends, during the regular holidays, and for the summer vacations. Parents are encouraged to visit the school regularly. There are private and public day schools, and private and public residential schools. A list of such schools is given in Chapter VIII.

The day school serves a community which is large enough to have a sufficient number of deaf children to make it possible to have such a school. If there are only a few children, all of different ages, the group activities which are so essential in the training of deaf children cannot be carried on satisfactorily. Whenever possible day schools should be establishd by communities in order that children may have the advantage of living at home.

Many communities are not large enough to have day schools. These communities are served especially by the residential school. Many of you find it difficult to enter your child in a residential school. You have much fear and apprehension about his being away from home. This is certainly understandable. However, unless suitable arrangements can be made in your community, it is unwise to provide just any kind of a program in order to keep your child at home. By developing a good attitude and by training your child well you can do a great deal to prepare him for entering any school, day or residential.

Perhaps the most satisfactory way to proceed if you have a choice of schools is to seek advice regarding the best school for your particular child. All children are different and have different needs. The school should be selected on the basis of your child's special needs and abilities. Also, when possible it is wise to visit the schools soon after learning that your child is deaf. Talk to the school authorities and give them an opportunity to assist you in planning your child's school program.

If your child has considerable residual hearing he may be able to enter a special or regular class in the regular public school for hearing children after he has had basic training in a special school. Usually this is possible only after speech and speech reading have been well established and if a hearing aid can be used.

There are many excellent schools for the deaf, both day and residential, private and public. For the best school program for your child it is essential that you and the school work together in harmony.

Chapter VII

WHAT TO EXPECT FROM
YOUR CHILD

$\mathcal{T}$he parents of a little deaf girl three years of age once asked us for advice regarding her training and education. After some discussion the father asked, "What do deaf people do? How do they get along in a highly complex and competitive society?" In our experience of consulting with a large number of parents this kind of question has been raised many times. After realizing that their daughter was deaf these parents became concerned about what should be expected of her. Never having had any real contact with deaf people, they had no experience on which to base their long-range plans.

It is wise to think far ahead, as these parents were doing. It is necessary to plan day by day, week by week, and year by year. Certain goals, certain expectations, and some plans can be made for five and ten years ahead. Such plans and expectations must be based on specific facts about your child. You can get information about him which will help you make such plans realistically.

For example, at about three years of age you can usually have a psychological examination to determine his mental capacity. Knowing whether he is below average, average, or above average mentally helps you in knowing how to handle him and in knowing what to expect from him. Likewise, an evaluation can be made of his social maturity. This is of help in knowing how he compares with other children in assuming responsibility and in learning how to care for himself. This was discussed in Chapter V. As he grows older and reaches adolescence the psychologist can determine his special aptitudes, such as mechanical and artistic aptitudes. This will help you to know what to expect from him as a worker in a particular occupation. Tests of muscular coordination can be given at an early age. These tests provide further information which is helpful in knowing whether he has other problems in addition to his deafness or whether his coordination is average or better than average. His personality and adjustment can be assessed and wise direction can be given. Only through an evaluation of all of his abilities and limitations can you know what to expect from your child and how best to plan for his future.

DEAF CHILDREN ARE NORMAL MENTALLY

For some time in years past, deaf children were thought to be retarded mentally. In recent years this has not been found to be true. When tests of intelligence which do not require language are used the deaf child is found to be equal to the hearing child. This does not mean that there are no deaf children with retarded intelligence. It means that deafness in itself is not an indication of mental inferiority. This is a significant fact. If most deaf children were also mentally retarded their handicap would be a double one; what they could be expected to achieve in school and in later life would be greatly reduced. From what we have learned about the intelligence of deaf children, if your child is typical you should expect him to be of average intelligence.

Likewise, deaf boys have been found to be equal to hearing boys in mechanical ability. The average deaf boy, if he is given comparable training, can do work requiring mechanical skill as well as the hearing boy of the same age.

DEAFNESS AND PERSONALITY

Perhaps you have heard people describe the deaf as being seclusive and suspicious. While scientific evidence to support this belief is not yet available, it is possible that becoming deaf in adolescence or later in life does tend to make one live more within himself and to become suspicious of others. However, this does not seem to be true of those who have been deaf from infancy. Children and adults who have been deaf from infancy do not have a certain type of personality. They are different, one from another, just as are people with normal hearing. Most of them are happy and have no real difficulty in getting along with others. Some are unhappy, have few friends, and find it hard to enjoy life. This means that there are all types of personalities and adjustments in a group of deaf people; deafness from early life does not in itself cause a certain type of personality to develop. This too is very important to you. It means that your child's personality will depend largely on your attitudes toward him and on how you train, guide, and direct him.

DEAFNESS AND SCHOOL ACHIEVEMENT

School achievement is dependent on ability to speak, to read, and to write. In Chapter VII we discussed the effect on communication of deafness in early life. The major consequence of deafness in infancy is the limitation it imposes on natural communication. As a result of this limitation the average deaf child is considerably retarded in school achievement as compared to the average hearing child of the same age. Presently even after completing his training in a special school the average deaf child is from two to three years retarded in his school work.

The average hearing child at 12 years of age is doing seventh to eighth grade work. The average deaf child at 12 years of age is doing fourth to sixth grade work. You should not be distressed by this comparison. Perhaps research and new methods of teaching will indicate ways of overcoming this educational retardation in the future. Furthermore, you must remember that this is the area in which the deaf child is most retarded; much is being accomplished by bringing about his present degree of school achievement. Not all deaf children are retarded educationally. A few, because of unusual brightness and other advantages, not only overcome this retardation but complete high school and college courses.

EARNING A LIVING

To be able to earn one's own living, to be mature, independent, and self-sufficient is the goal and ambition of all people. The deaf are not an exception. They want to be independent, to care for themselves; they do not want to be identified as objects of charity. They are ambitious, proud and industrious; they are entirely self-sufficient and self-supporting as a group. They earn their own living and they have good employment records.

Deaf children should have good vocational guidance and training. There are some kinds of work which they cannot do, but they are presently employed at a great variety of occupations. The occupations in which deaf people are working include engineering, photoengraving, floriculture, linotyping, watch and typewriter repairing, auto mechanics, power sewing machine operation, woodworking, upholstering, photography, chemistry, beauty culture, the ministry, teaching, and many other kinds of skilled and unskilled work.

You should not be apprehensive about your child's earning a living. There are many kinds of work which he can do. With realistic handling, good academic and vocational training, and expert guidance so that he will use his best abilities, he will take his place successfully in the world of work.

A HEARING WORLD

One of the main objectives for your child should be that he gradually, but realistically, recognize that he must live in a world where it is natural to hear. He should not only be aware that he must adjust to living and working with hearing people, but also that they will have certain negative attitudes toward him. Many hearing people think of the deaf as being peculiar and inferior. This is because the average individual is inclined to be somewhat afraid of people who are different from himself. People in general do not have more patience and tolerance for the deaf person. They may even have less patience and tolerance for a deaf fellow worker than they have for a hearing fellow worker. Often hearing people do not want to be associated with the deaf because they fear that they too will be considered strange and peculiar.

These attitudes of society, of the mass of hearing people, are a part of what it means to be deaf. Unfortunately the full importance of these attitudes is not yet fully recognized or understood. However, one way of understanding the problems which your child will face is to think of him as belonging to what is commonly referred to as a minority group. In a sense people will think negatively of him; he will be discriminated against because he is deaf. For example, deaf people have been refused the rental of a farm, a house, or an apartment because the landlord himself considered them inferior and incapable, or because he was afraid of what the neighbors would say. Some employers have said that they could not employ deaf people because hearing employees resented the fact that a deaf person could do the work as well as they. Apparently these hearing workers felt that their work suffered in prestige if it could be done equally well by a deaf person.

Part of the "art of being deaf" is to be aware that the public has these feelings and attitudes. Your child, as he grows up, must learn to understand hearing people. He must learn that their attitudes toward him come largely from fear, because they do not understand the deaf and the problem of deafness. He must by his attitude and manner demonstrate that he knows how they feel; he must help them to understand. Gradually he will be accepted by the people with whom he comes in contact. But because few hearing people include the deaf among their social friends or equals, it is wise for the deaf also to have deaf friends. A sense of belonging to a group is essential for real emotional satisfaction and happiness. All deaf people should have good hearing friends. However, often deaf friends who have common problems are more satisfying, more helpful and more genuinely worthwhile.

Perhaps you have not wanted your child to be identified with other deaf children. Perhaps you have not thought of his associating with deaf people as he grows up. Then perhaps you too need to examine your attitudes and to find out why you feel as you do. Remember it is essential that your child have real feelings of acceptance and of belonging to a group. Some deaf children and adults are not successful in really belonging to either the groups of the hearing or to the groups of the deaf. This is unfortunate. These are the deaf people who often have serious difficulties in getting along in life. You must be aware of the attitudes of society, aware of these broad and basic problems, in order to guide your child wisely. The world is not against you or against your child. People in general simply have not encountered the problem of deafness. By being sympathetic, tolerant, objective, and realistic, you can show your child how to meet and overcome these difficulties.

HELPING OTHER PARENTS

It is possible for you not only to do a great deal to help yourself and your child, but also to help other parents of deaf children. The technical work of teaching, medical treatment, fitting of hearing aids, psychological evaluation and research must be done by people especially trained for this work. But the main task of educating other parents and laymen must be given to you who are personally concerned about the problems of deafness. That is why parents' groups are being organized throughout the country. Such groups make it possible for you to discuss your mutual problems and for you to have lectures on specific subjects by known authorities. One of the most helpful and worthwhile steps that can be taken by parents who have recently

99

learned that their child is deaf is to join such a parents' group.

Many communities do not have parents' groups. Even if there are only a few parents scattered over a rather wide area in your community, it may be helpful to you and to the other parents to have discussion meetings. Also, more and more day and resi-

dential schools are organizing camps and developing parents' institutes. You can help other parents learn about and take part in these programs.

There is another way in which you can be helpful to all deaf children. You can become a well informed layman yourself and make it a point to inform other laymen about the problems of deaf children and adults. It is in this way that the negative attitudes we have discussed might be changed. A list of reading materials to help you become better informed is given in Chapter VIII.

You are the most important people in your child's life. You can do much for him but do not overlook the fact that you can be helpful to others who have problems like your own.

Chapter VIII

ORGANIZATIONS WHICH CAN HELP
——READING MATERIALS——
DIRECTORY OF SCHOOLS

*C*hapter VIII is divided into three parts: Part One includes a brief description of several organizations which can be of help to you. The officers and members of these organizations are familiar with the problems of children with impaired hearing. Whenever necessary you should contact them for assistance.

Part Two is a list of books and periodicals which contain help-ful suggestions on the training and development of deaf and hard of hearing children. One of your responsibilities is to be an informed parent. These readings will be of value to you in get-ting the background of information necessary for the best han-dling of your child.

Part Three is a directory of schools for the deaf and hard of hearing in the United States and Canada. You should begin early to plan your child's schooling. By going through this directory you can find the name and address of the school which is nearest you. Discuss your school plans with the authorities in your community.

PART ONE

Organizations which are particularly interested in providing information to parents of deaf and hard of hearing children

ORGANIZATIONS

AMERICAN HEARING SOCIETY, 817 14th St., N.W., Washington 5, D.C.
This Society functions through 115 chapters in many of which classes for parents are among the services offered. The goals of the national organization are prevention of deafness, conservation of hearing and rehabilitation of the hard of hearing. The Society distributes information on hearing, which includes many helps for parents. There may be a chapter in your community. Membership ($3.00) includes a monthly publication, *Hearing News*.

THE AUDIOLOGY FOUNDATION, 1104 S. Wabash, Chicago, Illinois.
An organization which sponsors research on deafness and training of specialists to work with the deaf and hard of hearing. It is interested in providing information and assistance to parents.

THE CONFERENCE OF EXECUTIVES OF AMERICAN SCHOOLS FOR THE DEAF and THE CONVENTION OF AMERICAN INSTRUCTORS OF THE DEAF, Gallaudet College, Kendall Green, Washington 2, D.C.
These organizations are for teachers and administrators who are actively engaged in educating the deaf in the United States and Canada. Information about schools and other questions will be furnished upon request. The official publication of these organizations is the *American Annals of the Deaf*.

THE INTERNATIONAL COUNCIL OF EXCEPTIONAL CHILDREN, National Education Association of the United States, 1201 Sixteenth Street, N.W., Washington 6, D.C.

This organization has chapters in many states and cities. There may be a chapter in your community. Information on the education and training of all types of exceptional children can be secured from Council members. The official publication is the *Journal of Exceptional Children.*

THE JOHN TRACY CLINIC, 924 W. 37th St., Los Angeles 7, California. This Clinic is noted for its work with parents of deaf children. It conducts a correspondence course for parents of preschool children. This course will be valuable to you in learning to work with your child. Parents may be enrolled upon application.

THE NATIONAL SOCIETY FOR CRIPPLED CHILDREN AND ADULTS, INC., 11 S. LaSalle St., Chicago 3, Illinois.
This organization is keenly interested in all types of exceptional children and their parents. It has affiliates in all 48 states, Alaska, Hawaii and Puerto Rico. Information on the deaf and hard of hearing will be sent upon request.

THE VOLTA BUREAU, 1537 35th St., N.W., Washington 7, D.C.
This Bureau is the headquarters for the Volta Speech Association and the editorial office for the *Volta Review.* It has the largest library on deafness in the world. The Volta Speech Association is an organization of parents, educators, and others interested in the deaf and hard of hearing. Its goal is to promote the teaching of speech and speech reading. Membership in this association would be valuable to you. Dues are $3 per year including a subscription to the *Volta Review.*

OTHER SOURCES OF INFORMATION

Most states have departments of special education. You can get information regarding facilities for the deaf and hard of hearing in your state and local community by writing to the officials in your State Department of Education. Many colleges and universities have Hearing Clinics, including services for parents.

Many states have departments of rehabilitation which provide services for the deaf and hard of hearing.

Local communities often have sources of information which may be overlooked. For example, the local and county superintendents of schools can furnish information on facilities and training of deaf and hard of hearing children. Your doctor and the county medical association also can be of help to you.

PART TWO

Books and periodicals which are especially helpful to parents of deaf and hard of hearing children

READING MATERIALS

BOOKS

Hearing and Deafness, A Guide for Laymen, edited by Hallo-well Davis. Murray Hill Books, Inc., 1947. $5
An excellent book which covers many aspects of deafness. It has much information which will be of value to you; written for the layman.

Opportunity and the Deaf Child, by Irene R. and Alex W. G. Ewing. University of London Press Ltd., 1947. $3
This book is directed to parents and teachers. Contains informa-tion on social training, speech reading, speech, and the education of the young deaf child. Has many suggestions for parents.

The Parents Manual, A Guide to the Emotional Development of Young Children, by Anna W. M. Wolf. Simon and Schuster, 1946. $2.75
This manual is a valuable guide for parents. It contains many helpful suggestions for handling unusual discipline and behavior problems.

The First Five Years of Life, A Guide to the Study of the Pre-school Child, by A. Gesell, *et al.* Harper, 1940. $4
This book is to be used as a guide to the physical and mental development of young children. It contains much helpful infor-mation for parents and professional workers.

The Pocket Book of *Baby and Child Care,* by Benjamin Spock. Pocket Books, Inc., 1946. $.35

Written for parents, this book contains a great deal of information on the physical care and habit training of young children.

PERIODICALS

American Annals of the Deaf, Editorial Office, Gallaudet College, Kendall Green, Washington, D.C.
The official publication of the Conference of Executives of American Schools of the Deaf and the Convention of American Instructors of the Deaf. A professional journal for educators of the deaf; articles on education and training.

Hearing News, Editorial Office, 817 14th St., N.W., Washington 5, D.C.
The official publication of the American Hearing Society. This bulletin carries professional articles on hearing aids, medical treatments, speech reading, auditory training, and other problems pertaining to the hard of hearing.

Journal of Exceptional Children, Editorial Office, Michigan State Normal College, Ypsilanti, Michigan.
The official publication of the International Council of Exceptional Children. A professional journal which includes articles on all types of exceptional children.

The Journal of Speech and Hearing Disorders, Editorial Office, 321 Illini Hall, University of Illinois, Urbana, Illinois.
The official publication of the American Speech and Hearing Association. A professional journal devoted to the technical problems of speech and hearing.

The Laryngoscope, Editorial Office, 640 S. Kingshighway, St. Louis 10, Missouri.
The official publication of the American Laryngological, Rhinological and Otological Society, Inc. A technical medical journal which carries articles on the treatment of deafness and the use of hearing aids.

Part Two

The Volta Review, Editorial Office, 1537 35th St., N.W., Washington 7, D.C.

The official publication of the Volta Speech Association. A monthly magazine which contains articles for both professional workers and parents. You can join the Volta Speech Association and receive the *Volta Review* regularly. The membership fee is $3.

PART THREE

*Schools for the deaf and the hard of hearing in the United States and Canada**

PUBLIC RESIDENTIAL SCHOOLS FOR THE DEAF IN THE UNITED STATES

School	Location
Alabama Institute for Deaf and Blind	Talladega, Ala. (205 E. South St.)
Alabama Institute for Deaf and Blind, Negro	Talladega, Ala. (Sylacauga Highway)
Arizona State School for the Deaf and the Blind	Tucson, Arizona
Arkansas School for the Deaf	Little Rock, Ark. (Markham & Park Sts.)
California	
California School for the Deaf	Berkeley 5, Calif. (Parker & Warring Sts.)
Sonoma State Home—Class for the Deaf	Eldridge, Calif.
California School for the Blind	Berkeley, Calif. (3001 Derby St.)
Class for the Deaf-Blind	Berkeley, Calif. (3001 Derby St.)
Colorado School for the Deaf and Blind	Colorado Springs, Colo.
Connecticut	
American School for the Deaf	West Hartford, Conn. (139 North Main St.)
Mystic Oral School for the Deaf	Mystic, Conn.
District of Columbia	
Columbia Institution for the Deaf	Kendall Green, Washington 2, D.C.
Kendall School for the Deaf	Kendall Green, Washington 2, D.C.
Gallaudet College	Kendall Green, Washington 2, D.C.
Florida	
Florida School for the Deaf and the Blind	St. Augustine, Fla. (San Marco Ave.)
School for Negro Deaf	St. Augustine, Fla. (San Marco Ave.)
Georgia School for the Deaf	Cave Springs, Ga.
Idaho State School for the Deaf and the Blind	Gooding, Idaho

*American Annals of the Deaf, January 1949

117

Public Residential Schools for the Deaf in the United States

Illinois School for the Deaf . . . . Jacksonville, Ill. (125 S. Webster Ave.)
Indiana State School for the Deaf . . . . . . Indianapolis 5, Ind. (1050 E. 42nd St.)
Iowa School for the Deaf . . . . Council Bluffs, Iowa
Kansas School for the Deaf . . . . Olathe, Kansas
Kentucky School for the Deaf . . . . . . Danville, Ky.
Louisiana
    State School for the Deaf . . . . Baton Rouge 2, La.
    State School for Deaf Negroes . . . . . Scotlandville, Baton Rouge, La. (Southern Univ.)
Maine School for the Deaf . . . . Portland 3, Maine (85 Spring St.)
Maryland
    State School for the Deaf . . . . Frederick, Md.
    School for the Blind, Dept. for Colored Deaf and Blind . Overlea, Baltimore 6, Md. (3800 Walnut Ave.)
Massachusetts
    Clarke School for the Deaf . . . . Northampton, Mass. (Round Hill)
    Beverly School for the Deaf . . . . . . Beverly, Mass. (6 Echo Ave.)
    Boston School for the Deaf . . . . Randolph, Mass. (N. Main St.)
    Michigan School for the Deaf . . . . . . Flint 2, Mich.
    Minnesota School for the Deaf . . . . . . Faribault, Minn.
Mississippi
    Mississippi School for the Deaf . . . . . Jackson, Miss. (1448 W. Capital)
    School for Negro Deaf . . . . Jackson, Miss. (1448 W. Capital)

Public Residential Schools for the Deaf in the United States

Missouri School for the Deaf	Fulton, Mo.
Montana School for the Deaf and the Blind .	Great Falls, Mont. (3800 2nd Ave. N.)
Nebraska School for the Deaf	Omaha 3, Nebr. (3223 N. 45th)
New Jersey School for the Deaf	West Trenton, N. J.
New Mexico School for the Deaf	Santa Fe, N. Mex. (1060 Cerrillos Road)
New York	
New York School for the Deaf . . .	White Plains, N. Y. (555 Knollwood Road)
St. Mary's School for the Deaf . . .	Buffalo 14, N. Y. (2253 Main St.)
Lexington School for the Deaf . . .	New York 21, N. Y. (904 Lexington Ave.)
St. Joseph's School for the Deaf . . .	New York, Bronx 61, N. Y.
Central New York School for the Deaf .	Rome, N. Y. (713 N. Madison St.)
Rochester School for the Deaf . . .	Rochester 5, N. Y. (1545 St. Paul St.)
North Carolina	
State School for the Blind and the Deaf, Negro School .	Raleigh, N. C. (Garner Road)
School for the Deaf	Morganton, N. C.
North Dakota School for the Deaf . . .	Devils Lake, N. Dak.
Ohio State School for the Deaf	Columbus 15, Ohio (450 E. Town St.)
Oklahoma	
School for the Deaf	Sulphur, Okla. (10th and Tahlequah)
State Institute for Deaf, Blind, and Orphans .	Taft, Okla.
Oregon State School for the Deaf . . .	Salem, Ore. (999 Locust St.)
Pennsylvania	
Pennsylvania School for the Deaf . . .	Mt. Airy, Philadelphia 19, Pa.

119

Public Residential Schools for the Deaf in the United States

Western Pennsylvania School for the Deaf . . . . . Edgewood, Pittsburgh 18, Pa.
Pennsylvania State Oral School . . . . . . Scranton 9, Pa. (1800 N. Washington Ave.)
Rhode Island School for the Deaf . . . . . Providence 6, R. I. (520 Hope St.)
South Carolina
  South Carolina School for the Deaf and the Blind . . Spartanburg, S. C.
  School for Negro Deaf . . . . Spartanburg, S. C.
South Dakota School for the Deaf . . . . . Sioux Falls, S. Dak. (E. 10th and Mable)
Tennessee School for the Deaf . . . . . Knoxville 15, Tenn. (Island Home Park)
Territory of Hawaii Diamond Head School . . . Honolulu 56, Hawaii (3440 Leahi Ave.)
Texas
  School for the Deaf . . . . Austin 22, Tex. (1102 S. Congress)
  Deaf, Dumb and Blind Institute for Colored Youths . Austin, Tex.
Utah Schools for the Deaf and the Blind . . . Ogden, Utah (846 20th St.)
Vermont, Austine School . . . . . . Brattleboro, Vt. (120 Maple St.)
Virginia
  School for the Deaf and the Blind . . . . Staunton, Va. (Beverly St.)
  Virginia State School . . . . Hampton, Va.
Washington State School for the Deaf . . . . Vancouver, Wash. (2901 E. 7th St.)
West Virginia
  Schools for the Deaf and the Blind . . . . Romney, W. Va.
  Schools for Colored Deaf and Blind . . . Institute, W. Va.
Wisconsin School for the Deaf . . . . . Delavan, Wis. (Walworth Ave.)

PUBLIC DAY SCHOOLS IN THE UNITED STATES

School	Location
California	
Eureka Day School	Eureka
Fresno Oral School	Fresno 11 (Fresno High School)
Long Beach Day School for the Deaf	Long Beach
Foshay Junior High School	Los Angeles 7
Mary E. Bennett School	Los Angeles 4
Frances Polytechnic High School	Los Angeles 15
Oakland Day School for the Deaf	Oakland 1
Pasadena Day School for the Deaf	Pasadena (McKinley Junior High)
Sacramento Day School for Deaf Children	Sacramento 16
San Diego, Oral Deaf Department	San Diego 3
Gough Oral School for the Deaf	San Francisco
San Jose Day School	San Jose
Colorado, Denver Day School for Deaf Children	Denver 3
Delaware, Class for Deaf, C. B. Lore School	Wilmington
Illinois	
Aurora Day School	Aurora
Champaign Day School for the Deaf	Champaign
Chicago	
Alexander Graham Bell School for the Deaf	3730 N. Oakley Ave. (18, Chicago)
Haines School, Classes for the Deaf	231 W. 23rd Place (7, Chicago)
Lake View High School, Dept. for the Deaf	4015 N. Ashland Ave. (13, Chicago)

Public Day Schools in the United States

Illinois (cont.)

Lane Technical High School, Deaf-Oral Dept. . . . . . . 2501 W. Addison St. (18, Chicago)
Mason School . . . . 1830 S. Keeler Ave. (23, Chicago)
Parker Elementary School for the Deaf . . . . . . 6800 Stewart Ave. (21, Chicago)
Parker High School, Deaf-Oral Department . . . . . 325 Normal Parkway (21, Chicago)
Perry School, Deaf-Oral Department . . . . . . 9128 University Ave. (17, Chicago)
Spalding School for Crippled Children, Deaf Department . . 1628 W. Washington Blvd.
Chicago Heights Day School . . . . Chicago Heights (Washington McKinley School)

East St. Louis Day School . . . . East St. Louis
Elgin Day School . . . . Elgin (Franklin School)
Elmhurst Day School . . . . Elmhurst (Lincoln School)
Evanston Day School . . . . Evanston
Joliet Day School for the Deaf . . . . Joliet
Moline Day School for the Deaf . . . . Moline
Rockford School for the Deaf . . . . Rockford (Henry Freeman School)
Winnetka Day School . . . . Winnetka

Iowa

Davenport Oral School for the Deaf . . . . . . Davenport
Smouse Opportunity School, Department for the Deaf . . . Des Moines 12
Sioux City Oral Day School for the Deaf . . . . . Sioux City 18
Kentucky, Deaf-Oral Classes, Louisville Public Schools . . . Louisville 8 (George H. Tingley School)
Louisiana, New Orleans Day School for the Deaf . . . . New Orleans 18

Public Day Schools in the United States

Maryland
 Baltimore Day School for the Deaf .   .   .   .   Baltimore 16
 Baltimore Day School for the Deaf, Colored Division .   .   Baltimore 23
Massachusetts
 Horace Mann School for the Deaf   .   .   .   .   .   Roxbury 19
 Lynn Day Class for the Deaf .   .   .   .   .   Lynn (Washington Community School)
 Springfield Class for the Deaf .   .   .   .   Springfield 5 (Elias Brookings School)
 Worcester Day Classes for the Deaf .   .   .   Worcester 4 (Upsala St. School)
Michigan
 Dearborn Public Schools Deaf Class .   .   .   .   Dearborn (Harvey H. Lowrey School)
 Detroit Day School for the Deaf, Main Branch and Eastern Unit .   Detroit 21
 Escanaba Oral-Deaf Class .   .   .   .   .   .   Escanaba
 Ferndale Oral Day School for the Deaf .   .   .   .   Ferndale 20
 Grand Rapids Oral School for the Deaf and Hard of Hearing .   Grand Rapids 6
 School for Exceptional Children, Unit for Deaf and Hard of Hearing   Hamtramck 12 (Pulaski School)
 Kalamazoo Day School for the Deaf and Hard of Hearing .   .   Kalamazoo 34 (Harold Upjohn School)
 Muskegon Oral Deaf School .   .   .   .   .   .   Muskegon
 Saginaw Oral Day School .   .   .   .   .   .   Saginaw
 Traverse City Oral Day School for the Deaf .   .   .   Traverse City
 Horace H. Rackham School of Special Education .   .   .   Ypsilanti (State Normal College)
Minnesota
 Duluth Day School for the Deaf .   .   .   .   .   Duluth 5
 Minneapolis Day School for the Deaf .   .   .   .   Minneapolis 8

Public Day Schools in the United States

Rochester Oral Day School for the Deaf . . . . Rochester
Jefferson School for the Deaf . . . . St. Paul
Central High School Speech Reading Class . . . . St. Paul
Missouri
Kansas City Day School for the Deaf . . . . Kansas City
Gallaudet Day School . . . . St. Louis 4
Turner School . . . . St. Louis 13
Nebraska, Lincoln Day School for the Deaf . . . . Lincoln 8
New Jersey
Bayonne Day School for the Deaf . . . . Bayonne
Jersey City Day School for the Deaf . . . . Jersey City
Newark School for the Deaf . . . . Newark 3
Paterson Day School for the Deaf . . . . Paterson 1
New York
Albany Conservation of Hearing Department . . . . Albany 3
Gloversville Day School for the Deaf and Hard of Hearing . . Gloversville 1 (Junior High School)
Junior High School, 47 Manhattan, New York Oral School . . New York 10
Public School 100, Queens . . . . 118th St., Ozone Park 16, N. Y.
Public School 40, Richmond . . . . Henderson & Lafayette Ave., S. I. 1, N. Y.
Ohio
Akron Day School for the Deaf . . . . Akron 11
Canton Public Day School for the Deaf . . . . Canton (Woodland School)

124

Public Day Schools in the United States

Cincinnati
   Oral School for the Deaf . . . . Cincinnati 8
   Deaf Class, Withrow Junior High School . . Cincinnati 8
   Alexander Graham Bell School . . . . . Cleveland 4
   Columbus Day School for the Deaf and Hard of Hearing . Columbus 1
   Kennedy School for the Deaf and Hard of Hearing . . Dayton 6
   East Cleveland School for the Deaf and Hard of Hearing . East Cleveland 12
   Franklin Day School for the Deaf and Hard of Hearing . Elyria
   Fremont School for the Deaf and Hard of Hearing . . Fremont
   Mansfield Day School for the Deaf . . . . Mansfield
   Portsmouth Day School for the Deaf . . . . Kinney's Lane
   Toledo, Lincoln School for the Deaf . . . . Toledo 6
   Youngstown Oral Day School for the Deaf . . . Youngstown
   Oklahoma, Tulsa Day School for the Deaf . . . Tulsa 6
   Oregon, Portland Day School for the Deaf . . . Portland 15
Pennsylvania
   Erie Day School for the Deaf . . . . . Erie
   Philadelphia, Willis and Elizabeth Martin School . . Philadelphia 4
   Tennessee, Memphis Oral Day School for the Deaf . Memphis (Bruce School Bldg.)
Texas
   Fort Worth Day School for the Deaf . . . . Fort Worth 4
   Houston Day School for the Deaf . . . . Houston 6

125

Public Day Schools in the United States

Virginia
Norfolk Day School for the Deaf . . . . . . Norfolk 6 (John Marshall School)
Richmond Day School for the Deaf . . . . . . Richmond 23
Washington
Seattle School for the Deaf . . . . . . Seattle (Summit School & John Marshall High)
Spokane School for the Deaf . . . . . . Spokane 9
Tacoma School for the Deaf and Hard of Hearing . . . Tacoma 5
W. Va., Huntington Oral School for the Deaf . . . Huntington 1
Wisconsin
Antigo Day School for the Deaf and Hard of Hearing . . Antigo
Appleton Department for Deaf and Hard of Hearing Children . Appleton
Eau Claire School for Atypical Children . . . . Eau Claire (First Ward School)
Green Bay Day School for the Deaf and Hard of Hearing . . Green Bay
Kenosha School for the Deaf and Hard of Hearing . . . Kenosha
La Crosse Day School for the Deaf and Hard of Hearing . . La Crosse
Madison School for the Deaf . . . . . . Madison (Lapham School)
Paul Binner School for the Deaf . . . . . . Milwaukee 2
Oshkosh Day School for the Deaf . . . . . . Oshkosh
Racine Day School for the Deaf and Hard of Hearing . . Racine (Henry Mitchell School)
Rice Lake Day School for the Deaf . . . . . Rice Lake (Lincoln School, Wilson Ave.)
Shorewood School for the Deaf . . . . . . Shorewood 11
Superior Day School for the Deaf and Hard of Hearing . . Superior
Wausau Day School for the Deaf . . . . . . Wausau

DENOMINATIONAL AND PRIVATE SCHOOLS IN THE UNITED STATES

School	Location
Alabama	
Montgomery School for the Deaf	Montgomery 2 (Oak Park School)
Birmingham Junior League School of Speech Correction, Inc.	Birmingham 3
California, John Tracy Clinic	Los Angeles 7
Florida, Sherman K. Smith School of Speech and Oral Education	Tampa 6
Georgia, Junior League School of Speech Correction, Inc.	Atlanta
Illinois, Ephpheta School for the Deaf	Chicago 41
Louisiana, St. Joseph Hall, Chinchuba Inst. for the Deaf	Marrero (Box 64)
Maryland, Reinhardt School for Deaf Children, Inc.	Kensington
Massachusetts	
Perkins Institution and Massachusetts School for the Blind, Dept. for Deaf-blind	Watertown 72
The Sarah Fuller Foundation for Little Deaf Children, Inc.	Roxbury 19
Michigan, Evangelical Lutheran Institute for the Deaf	Detroit 34
Minnesota, W. Roby Allen School	Faribault
Missouri	
Central Institute for the Deaf	St. Louis 10
St. Joseph Institute for the Deaf	University City 14
New York	
Cleary Oral School and Camp Peter Pan	Lake Ronkonkoma
New York Institute for the Education of the Blind, Dept. for Deaf-blind	New York 67
Wright Oral School	New York 28

Denominational and Private Schools in the United States

Ohio, St. Rita School for the Deaf	Lockland, Cincinnati 15
Oklahoma, Jane Brooks School for the Deaf . . .	Purcell
Pennsylvania	
Archbishop Ryan Memorial Institute for the Deaf . . .	Philadelphia 4
DePaul Institute for the Deaf	Pittsburgh 26
The Sanatorium School	Wawa
Puerto Rico, St. Gabriel's School for the Deaf . . .	Santurce 34
Texas, Dallas Pilot Institute for the Deaf	Dallas 9
Wisconsin, St. John's School for the Deaf	Milwaukee 7

SCHOOLS IN CANADA

School	*Location*
British Columbia School for the Deaf and the Blind .	Vancouver, B.C.
Nova Scotia—Halifax School for the Deaf . .	Halifax, N.S.
Ontario	
Hamilton Oral Classes for the Deaf .	Hamilton, Ontario
Ontario School for the Deaf . . .	Belleville, Ontario
Ottawa Class for the Deaf . . .	Ottawa, Ontario
Toronto Oral Day Classes for the Deaf .	Toronto
Toronto Preschool Classes . .	Toronto (King Edward School)
Quebec	
Institution Catholique . . .	Montreal 14, Quebec
Catholic Institute for Deaf Girls .	Montreal 18, Quebec
MacKay School for the Deaf . .	Montreal 28, Quebec
Saskatchewan School for the Deaf .	Saskatoon, Saskatchewan

INDEX

Activity, child's need for, 42, 43, 44, 45, 49
Aphasia, 9
Aptitudes, tests of, 94
Attitudes, 26, 27, 28, 31, 32, 33, 67, 80, 99
  consistency of, 36
  of acceptance, 28
  of indifference, 31
  of overprotection, 29, 30
  of remorse, 52
  of society, 98
  wishful, 30, 31
Audiogram, 79
Audiology, 5
Audiometer, 78 (*See also* Hearing, tests of)
Auditory training, 80, 81, 85, 86, 87, 88

Balance, 23, 69 (*See also* Semicircular canals)

Cochlea, 7

Communication, 48, 49, 50, 73, 75, 89, 95 (*See also* Language, Speech)
Consistency, in discipline, 36, 43, 63
  in feelings of success, 40, 41, 42
  in habit training, 54
  in showing affection, 36
  in sleep and rest, 71
  in talking to child, 36
  need for, 35
  of rules, 37

Deaf, age of becoming, 16
  child, 11, 12, 13, 17, 24, 27, 37, 38, 78
  children, 25
  definition of, 1, 2
  people, 4, 5, 25, 93 (*See also* Deafness)
Deafness, acquired, 19
  age of onset, 18, 76, 88
  and school achievement, 95, 96

Deafness—*Cont'd*
  conduction, 21
  congenital, 19
  causes and types of, 14, 15, 16,
    18, 19, 20
  degree of, 19, 76
  in the family, 5
  limitations caused by, 13, 23,
    31, 40, 41, 95
  nerve, 20, 23, 24
  psychological, 9
  treatment of, 16, 18, 20, 21, 47,
    48, 79
  true, 10 (*See also* Deaf)
Decibel, 8
Discipline, 27, 34, 36, 37, 39, 43,
    57, 61, 62, 63, 68

Ear, diagram of, 6
  inner, 6, 7, 20, 23
  middle, 6, 7, 21
  outer, 6, 7
Earaches, 21 (*See also* Medical
    treatment)
Eardrum, 6, 21
Employment, 96
Endogenous, 19
Etiology, 19
Eustachian tube, 7 (*See also* Ear,
    diagram of)
Exogenous, 19
Expression (*See* Speech, Com-
    munication)

Family, 13, 32, 40
  a wholesome, 40
  being a part of, 38, 39
  brothers and sisters, 39, 40, 44,
    45, 59, 62, 63, 65, 67
  relatives, 16

Fears, 65, 66
Fenestration operation, 22
Frequency, 8, 78, 79

Games, 41, 45
German measles, 19, 20

Habits, bedtime, 27, 70
  dressing, 27, 30, 55
  eating, 27, 30, 35, 53, 55, 57, 58
  toilet, 35, 51, 59, 60
  training of, 34, 41, 51, 52, 53,
    54
Hard of hearing, 1, 2
  children, 25 (*See also* Hearing,
    loss of)
Health (*See* Medical treatment)
Hearing, loss of, 5, 10, 11, 15, 19
  residual, 1, 73, 76, 77, 78, 80,
    83, 88, 92
  tests of, 7, 8, 76, 77 (*See also*
    Audiometer)
Hearing aids, 76, 78, 79, 80, 81,
    83, 84, 86, 87, 88, 89, 92
Hearing clinics, 5
Hearing impairment (*See* Hear-
    ing, loss of)

Independence, development of,
    45, 46, 47, 55, 96
Inner ear, 6, 7, 20, 23
Intelligence, 10, 24, 25, 94

Jealousy, 44, 63, 64, 67

Language, 16, 17, 35, 49, 53
Lip reading (*See* Speech reading)

Mechanical ability, 95
Medical treatment, 16, 18, 20, 21,
    47, 48, 79

Index

Meningitis, 23, 24
Mental ability, 10, 24, 25, 94
Middle ear, 6, 7, 21
Multiple handicaps, 24, 25

Nailbiting, 68
Neighbors, 71, 72

Occupations, 96
Organizations giving service and
    information, 105, 106
Otitis media, 21
Otosclerosis, 22

Parents groups, 99, 100
Personality, 13, 95
Pitch, 8, 78, 79
Psychological deafness, 9
Psychological examination, 94
Punishment (*See* Discipline)
Pure tone, 8, 79

Quarrelsomeness, 68

Reading materials for parents,
    111, 112

Schools, 89
    day, 91, 92
    directory of, 117
    for the deaf, 89
    nursery, 90
    residential, 91, 92
    special, 90
Screening tests, 79
Semicircular canals, 7, 23
Sleep and rest, 70
Social maturity, 94
Sound, 7, 8, 14, 16, 18, 35
Speech, 16, 17, 18, 48, 49, 73, 74,
    75, 79, 84, 85, 92
Speech reading, 50, 73, 75, 81, 82,
    83, 84, 85, 86, 88, 89, 92
Stubbornness, 68

Temper tantrums, 66, 67
Thumbsucking, 68
Toys, 45

Vocational guidance, 96
Voice (*See* Speech)

Walking, 23, 69

YOUR DEAF CHILD is a monograph in AMERICAN LECTURES IN OTO-LARYNGOLOGY, edited by Norton Canfield, M. D., Associate Professor of Otolaryngology, Yale University School of Medicine, New Haven, Connecticut

ABOUT THE AUTHOR

Dr. Myklebust received his A. B. from Augustana College in 1933 and his M. A. in the education of the deaf from Gallaudet College in 1935. He was a teacher in the Tennessee School for the Deaf from 1935 to 1939. He then became Director of Research and Child Study at the New Jersey School for the Deaf. At this time he began his study of clinical psychology and received his M. A. in this field from Temple University in 1943 and his Ed.D. from Rutgers University in 1945. At the present time he is Professor of Audiology and Director of the Children's Hearing Clinic at Northwestern University. He is a member of the American Psychological Association and a Diplomate in Clinical Psychology. Dr. Myklebust's articles on the psychology of the deaf child have appeared in such journals as the *American Annals of the Deaf, Journal of Speech and Hearing Disorders, Journal of Consulting Psychology*, and the *Volta Review*.

Reviews of Previous Printings . . .

"This book is written expressly for the parents of deaf children and can be enthusiastically recommended for its authoritative background, excellent writing, and thorough coverage of the problems associated with hearing impairment in childhood. There is constant emphasis on parental understanding as a prerequisite to normal personality development in the handicapped child . . . the publisher's usual high standard of book presentation adds even more stature to this fine volume."

— American Journal of Diseases of Children

"Certainly this book should be useful to parents of deaf children in clarifying their own attitudes and obtaining a better insight into the psychodynamics of deafness. Any book that reduces parents' confusions and conflicts makes its own contribution. Moreover, the book is simply written and should be understood by most parents without too much difficulty . . . surely, people with hearing losses, parents of deaf children, and workers in the field would neglect this book only at their own peril."

— The Crippled Child

CHARLES C THOMAS • PUBLISHER • SPRINGFIELD • ILLINOIS

ISBN 0-398-03127-4

American Lecture Series